MODERN
RADIO
PROGRAMMING

No. 623
$9.95

MODERN RADIO PROGRAMMING

By J. Raleigh Gaines

TAB BOOKS
Blue Ridge Summit, Pa. 17214

FIRST EDITION

FIRST PRINTING— MARCH 1973

Copyright ©1973 by TAB BOOKS

Printed in the United States
of America

Hardbound Edition: International Standard Book No. 0-8306-3623-4

Library of Congress Card Number: 72-94807

Preface

I've felt for a long time that there is an enormous shortage of books on radio programming. For much too long, there have been too few books—almost none—on radio programming. The reasons are many, but mostly because there are too few people qualified to write such a book. Not necessarily because they do not know enough about programming a radio station, but because most of them don't know how to say the things they know. Some of them are even **afraid** to put what they know into words, for fear that it might thus disappear from their grasp or that someone who knows "one thing more" can thus beat them in combat. And, I assure you, programming competition today is war. Even one thing, one esoteric little gimmick or contest can mean the difference in winning or losing. In one smaller market a few years ago, one Top 40 station lost out on the ratings battle because contest fans couldn't find a buried treasure. The legend has always persisted that the competing Top 40 station program director, following the clues announced over the air, went out and dug the treasure up himself one night.

Phil (Bill Drake) Yarbough may tell you a different story, if you're ever lucky enough to get him to talk. He is one of the quiet ones. He once told too much to a certain program director and the young gentleman shortly afterwards went to work on the competing Top 40 station and knocked off one of the stations that Bill Drake consults.

Grahame Richards, a veteran Top 40 air personality and program director who grew to become general manager of a major market classical music station, once told me (after I'd plied him with a couple of drinks) that success in radio programming is often a matter of little, simple things. He prefers to identify a record before it's played and afterwards.

His reason is that he doesn't want to take the chance that someone might grow irritated because they didn't hear the name of the tune.

Bill Drake prefers that his air personalities come out of the news directly into music, and it has to be a familiar tune, preferably a past hit. Like many other program directors in Top 40 radio, Bill Drake considers the news basically a "tune-out" factor.

On a progressive rock station programmed by Jerry Stevens, you will probably never be told that you're listening to progressive rock music. A few country music stations today never tell their listeners that they're listening to country music. A very successful middle-of-the-road station in one of the nation's top 20 markets hasn't ever told its audience that they are listening to rock 'n roll, once a dirty word among MOR people. Wink Martindale, air personality on KMPC in Los Angeles, usually doesn't bother to mention that the old record he happens to have on the air at any particular time was a former "teenybop" hit.

Truly, the modern program director considers these and many more "nuances" his tools in trade. But, at the same time, there are certain "basics" in programming that are, perhaps, even more important. And to tell the truth, while none has written of the nuances in programming, very few people at all have written of programming—period.

J. Raleigh Gaines, a veteran air personality and program director under the name of Bob Raleigh, knows all the basics and, I believe, a large majority of the nuances. He paid his programming dues in all sizes of cities, under all kinds of conditions. And he has, in the past, shown a definitive interest in the broadening of programming knowledge. A few years ago, he promoted and organized a couple of regional southeastern meetings of general managers, program directors, and air personalities. I attended the first meeting, and it was a damned fine get-together.

In a sense, J. Raleigh Gaines and I have the same instinct within us—the preservation and the improvement of radio. We feel that the radio station in Brady, Texas, or Carlsbad, New Mexico, or Lexington, Kentucky should be almost as good in sound (certainly those stations should be **better** in service to the community) as the station with the same format in Dallas, Miami, or Seattle.

What I'm trying to say is that regardless of how good a program director may think he is, he could be better. It's up to the wise program director to seek and ferret out knowledge in any way, shape or possibility. One general manager, Art Simmers of WTRY in Troy, New York, occasionally takes his program director on a trip into a major market — just to listen to the more successful stations. Ordinarily, most program directors can't afford to do that sort of thing. And that's why this book by J. Raleigh Gaines (Bob Raleigh) could prove to be your closest friend. I certainly consider Bob to be a good friend of mine. And I heartily recommend this book to you, be you program director, disc jockey, manager, or college student.

Claude Hall
Radio-TV Editor
The Billboard Magazine

Contents

Fantasy—Image Transfer—Quickie Commercial—"Hot" Property Commercial—Improvisation Commercial—The Funny Commercial—Where Do Commercial Ideas Come From?—File Your Good Commercials—One Final Thought

Introduction

During a recent 6-month period, Billboard Magazine and other trade publications reported over 300 different notices of personnel and position changes within the radio industry. Nearly 35 percent of these changes were connected with the position of program director. This 35 percent figure does not indicate whether the change from one station to another was voluntary or involuntary. However, from personal contact with many of those individuals concerned, I would venture to guess that better than 50 percent of the changes could be directly related to (a) the failure of the program director to manage the people under him, (b) the failure of the program director to manage (get along with) the people over him, (c) the failure of the program director to cope with the day-to-day problems of his job, or (d) the failure of the program director to really comprehend the range and the depth of his responsibilities. In retrospect, we could very easily apply these same reasons for failure to disc jockeys, sales managers, salesmen, engineers, secretaries, and in some cases, even general managers.

Any one, or any combination, or all of the aforementioned reasons for failure stem basically from the lack of a working knowledge of the craft. At this moment I can name you 50 program directors across the country who are considered "tops" in their field. These 50 program directors (the number could well be several hundred) move from station to station purely on their ratings record which, in many cases, does not give the true picture of a program director's ability. And as they move, their "inabilities" sooner or later catch up with them. It's ironic that in almost all cases, the inability of a program director is blamed on the general manager with such glowing cop-outs as, "He wouldn't let me do my thing," or "I left because the management didn't know what it was doing," or "He'll get his. The station can't do without me."

I know one bright young man who worked at three major market stations, all within 18 months, and was "dismissed" from all three stations. In each instance his station's ratings were good and on the surface you would think that the management of each station must truly be crazy. But after a short conversation with this young gentleman, I discovered that he was a major market program director who had no understanding of cost controls or budgets. He didn't even know how to properly interpret a rating book. Yet, to this day, he still believes he was shafted three times.

By the same token, a similar young man started out as a DJ in one of the major southern markets. He worked his way up to one of the top ten markets and eventually found himself as program director of one of the country's leading rockers. But his inabilities caught up with him and it was only a question of time. Within six months, this young genius had held four top program director jobs and lost all of them. To the young man's credit, I should mention that at this writing he is the program director of a fine medium market station in the south, and in our last conversation he was "learning his trade." There is no doubt in my mind that this PD will be back up in the big time. He analyzed his problem and went to work to solve it.

Also, it is a fact that many of the people coming out of college and broadcasting schools are totally unprepared to face the responsibilities of modern broadcasting. Of course, there are some fine colleges and broadcasting schools who perform a great service and do a creditable job of teaching. However, there are also many who are either not interested enough, or qualified, to teach radio. The very sad fact is that most colleges either concentrate in the area of television or have radio courses taught by professors who still think a "cluster" has something to do with astrology and a "sweep" is something the janitor does in the control room every night. Unfortunately, the broadcast schools are not in any better shape. Most of them are just factories who take almost anyone, as long as they can read, write, and "have the tuition."

There are some very good broadcast schools that offer a very solid radio course, but there are no guidelines to enable a prospective student to recognize those that are accredited and those that are out for a fast buck.

Within the radio industry today, the simple truth is that most program directors are really just glorified music directors. Or perhaps I should say, just music directors with the title of program director. And most disc jockeys are just button pushers who sit around all day waiting to be discovered, or worse yet, sit around and congratulate themselves on how talented they are.

Thus, the reason for this book. To give program directors, disc jockeys, and students more insight into their position and responsibilities. I could very easily have entitled this book "How To Keep Your Job." Because this is the true purpose of the book.

The procedures, systems, suggestions, and opinions set forth in this chronicle are not intended to be the answer to all problems in radio. It is hoped the material will stimulate you into devising your own systems and procedures in order to become a more effective and more knowledgeable person, or, to put it more bluntly, to insure your job. The more effective you are, the less chance the station will decide to proceed without your services.

So, if I may make a suggestion: **Read this book.** Study the material. Let your mind be stimulated. And allow yourself to become not an imitator but an innovator!

What Is a Program Director?

Ask any ten people, "What is a program director?" and you'll get ten very wordy and very detailed definitions. I, for one, prefer the definition that is set forth in the policy manual prepared by a large southern group operation. This manual defines the program director, very simply, as the individual who has the basic responsibility of relieving the general manager of headaches. How much simpler can a definition be? **To relieve the general manager of headaches.** That, in its purest form, is the job of the program director. If the general manager's only headaches originate from within the sales department, you are doing your job. And your job is a position of trust. A position of trust with the public, true; but more important, the program director has a position of trust with management. Violate that trust and you suddenly find that you are an ex-program director.

Before we go any further, let's take a test. Over the years, I have developed a rating or evaluation system for use on myself and on program directors of stations I have consulted. I'm sure that after you have reviewed the test, you will be able to improve it. However, the important thing is to be as honest and as objective as you possibly can. The only person who will suffer from a lack of objectivity is the person taking the test. After having completed the test, I am sure there will be improvements that can be made. I would suggest that you keep a copy of this test in your brief case and, from time to time, evaluate yourself. Sometimes it can be a real eye-opener.

This test, however, is not restricted to program directors only. Any DJ who has aspirations of becoming a manager should, from his very first day in radio, begin to acquaint himself with the problems and responsibilities of management. Even if a DJ has no desire or talent to move into the management field, it behooves him to know as much about his profession as possible. In a later chapter there is a Disc Jockey Evaluation Test, but we must still remember that radio is a business and, therefore, each person should learn every aspect of that business. So, if you are a disc jockey, take both tests.

The Program Director's Rating and Evaluation test is divided into ten basic categories with sub-categories in each. A maximum of one hundred points is available in each category and each sub-category is rated according to importance. Upon completion of the test, add your points in each category. Then add all ten totals and divide by ten. This will, of course, give your grade or average. The grading guidelines following the test will give you an idea of how you rate as a program director. Remember, it is important—only to you—that you be objective and honest in your own evaluation.

PROGRAM DIRECTOR'S RATING AND EVALUATION

1. Management Abilities	Maximum Points	Rating
A. FCC rules awareness. How well are you up on the latest rules and regulations?	20	——
B. Cost control awareness. Are you constantly on the watch for money-wasting practices in your department? Do you operate within your prescribed budget? Do you watch expenses and overtime?	20	——
C. Personal adherence to company policy. Do you follow all directives from the front office or do you occasionally deviate?	10	——
D. Personnel adherence to company policy. How well do the people under you follow company policy? Do they follow it to the letter or		

do they know that occasionally you are inclined to turn your head? · 10 · —

E. Delegation of duties. Do you assign specific duties to people under you or are you mostly inclined to go ahead and do it yourself? · 20 · —

F. Advance planning. How much advance planning do you do? Do you program from day to day, week to week, or month to month? · 20 · —

Total · —

2. On-Air Programming

A. Music control. Do you have absolute control over the records played or is it left to the DJ's discretion? · 10(or 0) · —

B. Awareness. Does the station sound as if it knew what was going on in the market? · 10 · —

C. Public service and public affairs. Do you rely on syndicated programs and announcements or do you initiate and broadcast local PA and PSAs? · 20 · —

D. Quality of air sound. Does the station sound "flow," or does it have a jerky sound? Is it correct in a technical sense? · 10 · —

E. DJ ad lib control. Do you have some control over what the jocks say or can they just "wing" it? · 10 · —

F. DJ administrative control. Do your jocks maintain their logs properly at all times or do you have to constantly get after them? · 10 · —

G. DJ execution. Do your jocks implement your policies or do they devitate, knowing that you don't police the sound too well? — **10** — ——

H Music research. Do you personally oversee all music research or do you rely solely on trade reports for information on what you play in your market? — **10** — ——

I. Jingles, promotion spots, etc., control. Do you have or maintain absolute control or do the jocks wing it? — **10** — ——

Total — ——

3. Administration

A. Production. Do you have a systematic procedure for all personnel to follow in regards to producing commercials? — **30** — ——

B. Tape save system. Do you have a system whereby you can place your hands on any tape (jingle, commercial, or past program) on a moment's notice or do you have to stop and hunt for it? — **20** — ——

C. Copy file system. Is there a system of filing copy whereby anyone can place his hands on any given piece of copy for any date, or is a massive hunt necessary to find what you're looking for? — **10** — ——

D. Log save system. Are logs systematically checked for errors and systematically corrected and then filed for easy reference? — **20** — ——

E. Out-of-market correspondence. Do you respond quickly to agency queries and requests? Do you handle all correspondence in a speedy manner?   5   ——

F. In-market correspondence. How speedily do you respond to correspondence from listeners, sponsors, etc?   5   ——

G. Suspense file system. Do you maintain and check a suspense file?   5   ——

H. Interoffice memos and file. Do you react or respond immediately to interoffice memos and do you maintain a handy reference file for them?   5   ——

Total   ——

4. Station Community Involvement

A. Local public service. Do you just schedule enough PSAs to meet your FCC requirements or do you run enough to insure results?   20   ——

B. Local public affairs. Do you just run your requirements or do you seek out areas in which the station may assist the community?   20   ——

C. Quality of public service. Are announcements of the "knockout" variety or do you really produce them?   20   ——

D. Quality of public affairs programs. Do you just schedule and broadcast or do you really make an effort to develop programs above the average?   20   ——

E. Personal involvement in the community. Are you involved in the community (belong to clubs, organizations) or do you just operate from your desk?   10   ——

F. Community awareness. Do you keep a suspense file on upcoming community events and projects or is it necessary for the club publicity chairman to advise you on various projects and activities?   10   ——

Total   ——

5. Programming Creativity

A. Programming research. Do you read all trade magazines and reports for new programming ideas regularly? Do you correspond with other program directors regularly to exchange programming ideas and concepts?   30   ——

B. Idea bank file. Do you maintain a file of good ideas for possible future use or do you just rely on your memory? Do you refer to this file on a regular basis?   20   ——

C. Flexibility. Are you able to adjust a new idea to your market or do you follow what the other station did?   10   ——

D. Execution. Are you just an idea man, unable to implement your ideas, or do you carefully carry them out to their completion?   20   ——

E. Ability to improve an idea. Can you take an idea from another program director and improve on it, innovate?   20   ——

F. Originality and cleverness in this category is worth an additional 10 points. Are you original and clever?   10   ——

Total   ——

6. Commercial Creativity

A. Submission of commercial ideas. Do you regularly submit ideas for commercials or sales to the sales department or do they have to wring one out of you?   30   ——

B. Commercial idea research. Do you regularly seek out new ideas for commercials or sales utilizing RAB, trade magazines, monitoring, etc.?   30   ——

C. Execution of commercial ideas. Are you able to follow up on your ideas or are you content with just giving birth?   30   ——

D. Personnel involvement. Are the people under you involved to the extent that they submit new commercial or sales ideas? Or do they just assume an I don't really care attitude?   10   ——

E. Originality and cleverness in commercial creativity is worth an additional ten points. Are you a good commercial idea man?   10   ——

Total   ——

7. Promotional Creativity

A. Promotion and contest research. Do you seek out new promotion or contest ideas or are you content to just wait for one to drop in your lap?   20   ——

	Maximum Points	Rating

B. Promotional idea bank file. Do you maintain and refer regularly to a file of promotion and contest ideas? **20** ___

C. Ability to improve an idea. Can you? **10** ___

D. Advance planning. Do you plan and coordinate your ideas weeks in advance or do you initiate and implement at the last moment? **20** ___

E. Execution. How well do you execute and carry out your ideas? **30** ___

Total ___

8. Follow-Up Aptitude

A. Execution of your own ideas. Do you carry out your own ideas and instructions? **10** ___

B. Execution of the manager's instructions. Do you immediately carry out his instructions or do you dilly-dally? **20** ___

C. Execution of sales requests. Do you respond immediately to requests from the sales department? **20** ___

D. Memo and letter follow-up. Do memos and letters get priority attention from you or do you procrastinate? **10** ___

E. Handling of small details. Are you in the habit of putting off bothersome and petty details or do you handle them immediately? **40** ___

Total ___

9. Neatness of Station

A. Control room **10** ___

B. Program director's office **30** ___

	Maximum Points	Rating
C. Production studios	10	——
D. Desks	5	——
E. Newsroom	5	——
F. Files	20	——
G. Personnel	20	——
Total		——

10. Personnel Relations

A. The ability to get the job done with a minimum of fuss with the staff	30	——
B. The ability to get along with people. Does not necessarily mean are you buddy-buddy, rather that you have a congenial relationship with your staff.	10	——
C. Capable of getting the needed cooperation from the program staff?	10	——
D. Getting along with sales staff. Do you work with the sales staff or do you have a constant battle underway?	25	——
E. Good working relationship with other station personnel?	10	——
F. Station enthusiasm. Is the morale high with your staff? Or low?	15	——
Total		——

Well, how did you rate? If you scored between 100 and 90, you're outstanding. If your score was between 89 and 76, you are an above average program director. Now, to the embarassing part. If your final rating was 75 to 60, you are only average. And if your score falls between 59 and 40, there is definite room for improvement. Any score of 39 or below is just not acceptable and it means that it is time for you to either buckle down and learn your trade or get a job selling shoes to fat little ladies with charge cards.

If you really want to be objective in this test, I suggest that you have your general manager perform the rating. In all the years I've used this evaluation system, not once did I truly get an objective rating from a program director. This fact holds true for me also. It is human nature to overrate ourselves or to admit knowing (or thinking we know) more than we really do. So, just for kicks, have the general manager rate you. You may get a real shock. And perhaps that shock will enable you to take a more analytical look at your performance.

Within the next chapters, we cover the subjects mentioned in the evaluation. If you scored well on the test (and if your general manager gave you a good rating) you may just want to put this book down and go sit in the sun and dream of the day when Bill Drake or Ken Draper will be pleading for your advice. However, if your score was in the lower category, I urge you to read on. Who knows. Maybe you'll learn something.

The Program Director— A Member of the Management Team

Many years ago a program director in the Storz Chain told me that if you wanted to be a successful program director, the jocks had to know you were the boss. He further stipulated that it was a good idea to remember that boss spelled backwards was double sob. I mention this for only one reason. Once you accept a position of program director, you cease to be "one of the boys." From the moment you become the program director, you are a part of the management team. Or to put it a little more strongly, you become one of the bosses.

There are very few program directors who can be one of the boys after office hours and be a successful boss during working hours. It just can't be done. When you move into management, your entire outlook and perspective must change. If you think you can be one of the boys and also a program director, chances are that in the very near future you will suddenly become an ex-program director at that particular station.

Earlier we mentioned that as a program director you have a trust. To retain and maintain this trust, you must act in the manager's and station's best interest. If this requires you to be a boss spelled backwards at times, well, that's part of the job. And your job is to help manage the radio station. Or to be more specific, to fade the general manager.

Far too many program directors honestly believe (perhaps I should say mistakenly believe) that their responsibilities are primarily concerned with the sound of the station. Well, there are a few more that you should be aware of.

Take for example, **awareness of the FCC Rules and Regulations.** This is probably the most basic of all the program director's immediate duties. And yet you can pick up

PROGRAMMING COMMITMENT SCORECARD

PA—1 percent (1.7 hrs.)

Sun: 6 PM Georgetown Forum (30)

Sun: 9 PM Local Forum

OTHER — 3 percent (5 hrs.)

Sun: 9:30 PM Univ. Forum (30)

Sun: 10 PM Univ. Talent (30)

Mon: 10 PM Powerline (30)

Tues: 10 PM Congressman Smith (15)

Tues: 10 PM Silhouettes (30)

Wed: 10 PM Teen Show (60)

Sun: 6 AM Rev. Smith (30)

6:30 AM Rev. Jones (30)

7 AM Rev. Ray (30)

7:30 AM Rev. Black (30)

11 AM 1st. Baptist Church (60)

Thurs: 8 PM NASA (5)

Sat: 6 AM Health & You (30)

NEWS — 6 percent (10 hrs.)

24 4-min casts per day X 7 days.

+

1 15-min at 12 noon every day

Note: This scorecard may also be used as a weekly checklist to insure that each tape is in its proper place and available to the announcer at broadcast time. (The percentages are based on a 168-hour week.)

any copy of "Broadcasting Magazine" and read about a station being cited for improper logging, a station operating without a properly licensed operator, and I could go on and on. The point here is that the program director should insure that a station is operating according to regulations. Now, don't give me some guff that engineering should look after their end, traffic should be concerned with logging, sales should be aware of how many commercials are being aired. A program director's responsibilities encompass all of these departments. It is the responsibility of the program director to insure, or at least be aware, that these departments are functioning up to snuff.

I could devote the better part of this book to just FCC rules and regulations. However, I think a touch on base will suffice. To begin with, be aware of your station's FCC commitments. How about a quick question or two? Without stopping to think, how many public service announcements is your station supposed to schedule every week? What percentage of your weekly programming is dedicated (or committed) to public affairs? To "Other"? To News? If you can't come up with a quick and true answer, now would be a very good time to make a mental note to check your station license to obtain the answers!

I've always made it a policy to keep this information right at my fingertips. A five-by-eight card under the glass on your desk (or at least where you can see it every day) will serve as a constant reminder. List the categories, the programs, the length of each program, and the time and day that program is broadcast. (See the sample "scoreboard.") You might also want to consider the idea of carrying more than your commitment. At least 30 minutes more. The reason is that if you are using taped programs from an out-of-town source, the first time a tape is delayed, in the mails for instance, your commitment for that week is going to be deficient. Therefore, by carrying over your commitment, you're always relatively safe.

Secondly, keep up to date on the latest rules changes and interpretations. If your station retains a Washington lawyer, the station probably receives a memo from the lawyer, periodically. Make it a point to read these memos. It's also a very good practice to post such memos on the bulletin board and require the jocks to read them. If your station does not retain a lawyer who provides you with periodic memos, let me suggest that you read "Broadcasting Magazine" each week. The magazine always reports the latest news from the Commission, including the report on who got fined for what.

Thirdly, as the program director it is your responsibility to insure that the program logs are filled out properly. More stations get "gigged" for improper logging procedures than any other one infraction. And it's really such a simple matter to prevent the violation in the first place. The best policy, I've found, is to check the log daily and have the corrections made that very same day. If you wait, you'll just end up behind the eight ball. By checking and correcting the program logs on a daily basis, you eliminate the potential problem of losing a jock before the logs are corrected, thereby leaving you with an incorrect log and no one to make the proper correction. It's a good idea to check with your engineer to insure that the transmitter logs are being maintained properly, also. Of course, it is his primary responsibility, but you are still part of the management team—dedicated to fading your general manager.

Last, but certainly not least in importance, is insuring against overcommercialization. This is a tough area to enforce, particularly if you are in the small or medium markets. However, a violation in this area can be serious. Check your license to find out what your maximum hourly load can be and then make sure you stay at, or within, that limit. Your traffic director is primarily responsible for this department, but it is imperative that you provide a double check. And the most simple double check is the announcer on duty. Get the announcers into the habit of counting each hour's commercials prior to running the schedule. If the count is over the maximum allowed, you should have a procedure ready for the announcer to follow to bring the count back to where it should be. And when making your count, be sure to add that network news commercial. It counts and many people fail to take it into consideration. That could be the one commercial to throw your entire hour off. Watch for over commercialization very closely.

COST CONTROL PRACTICES

How often have you heard the expression, "The name of the game is sales." Well, the next time you hear this rather redundant statement, make a correction. The name of the game is profits! Stockholders will always be impressed with a steadily climbing sales graph, but their real joy and ecstasy is derived from that final entry on the bottom of a profit and loss statement. Profit spells bonus, raises, better equipment, and better salaries for you and your people. No matter how good the sales picture might be, the key to a successful operation is cost control. Keep the expenses down and you keep the profits up. And when the profits are up, the front office will be more receptive to your ideas, wants, and needs. You may be the most creative, most imaginative program director to ever come down the pike, but if you can't master the art of keeping costs and expenses down, you will very quickly become an untrusted albatross around the manager's neck.

There are many ways you can help keep the costs down. And I immediately want to make clear that cutting salaries or starting jocks out at a lower than normal salary is not my idea of cutting costs. We'll explore this particular area in depth in a later chapter.

My idea of keeping the costs down revolves primarily around normal programming administrative functions. For example, the telephone. Alexander Graham Bell's brain child has been the undoing of many a program director. It is so easy to just pick up the phone and call a record man or your buddy under the guise that it is strictly in the best interest of the station to make a call. Stop and think. Is a one dollar record worth a three dollar phone call? If you really need the record, call the record company collect. If you're not important enough for them to accept a collect call, you better start doing some public relations work with that company. However, respect their cost control problems also. A letter with an eight cent stamp will more than likely get there over night and you'll have what you want within a day or two. You'll find that the company will respect you for it. And then when you really do need to call, a collect call will be no problem. The mail system will also keep you out of hot water in staying in contact with your buddies. I like to think of the telephone as my enemy. It's sitting on my desk, a constant temptation. I've seen company presidents and auditors get more bent out of shape over a high telephone bill than on any other single expenditure. Granted, the telephone is a necessity. However, bear in mind that the telephone can also be a luxurious detriment to your job. Keep the telephone calls to a bare minimum.

Watch your stationery and office supplies, too. These are items that can quickly get out of control. Magic Marker pens, ball point pens, Scotch tape, letterheads, tablets, and the like can run your yearly programming budget right out of sight. Keep some sort of control on these items. Just as managers can lose their cool over the telephone bill, a note from a jock to the program director on a station letterhead will accomplish pretty much the same thing. I always made it a policy to never buy note tablets of any type for any reason. There is a less expensive way. Grab a box of Teletype paper and carry it to a printer. He'll cut it to any size you specify and you'll have enough note pad paper to last a year. It's perfect for the news department (on a clip board and as news copy paper), for the jocks to use as scratch paper, and I even know of some stations that use Teletype paper as copy paper (saving on that yearly copy paper printing bill).

How many records are you buying every month? No matter what type of service you may be getting from the record companies, it can always be improved by a little public relations work on your part. Improve your record service and cut down the cost of buying them. Short notes to the distributors and record promotion men will accomplish miracles in getting records. All they ask is that you take an interest in their product. And if you take an interest in them, they will, in turn, take an interest in you.

If some of these suggestions sound cheap, think again! Everytime you show the manager how you're saving a buck, your stock with him goes up a few points. Get enough points and you're in a pretty good bargaining position for a raise or even a bonus.

Be creative and imaginative in your cost control efforts. Don't, of course, let it become an obsession with you, but do keep an eye out for ways to cut expenses. When the expenses are down, the profits are up and your manager will look good in the eyes of the stockholders. And when he looks good, you look good.

PERSONAL AND PERSONNEL ADHERENCE TO COMPANY POLICY

The biggest and most common mistake made by young program directors is copping out with the staff. Sometimes when a directive is issued by the manager, a program director will occasionally reveal a negative attitude—in the presence of his staff—by saying, "Well, here it is. I don't agree with it but this is the way the boss wants it and I guess we better humor him and do it his way." **Mark this well.** When a directive comes from the manager's office and it becomes your responsibility to enforce that directive, then you had better remember what we stated earlier: You have a position of trust with the manager. That directive literally becomes your directive, whether you're in favor of it or not. It is your prerogative—and duty—to argue the merits of the directive with the manager; however, it is also your duty to never discuss or argue the merits of the directive with the staff or in front of the staff. I have to repeat this bit of advice. A directive from the manager's office is the same, as far as your staff is concerned, as if it were your own directive. And once that directive has been issued, you then not only have the responsibility of carrying out that directive, but you are obliged to comply with that directive yourself. You can't very well expect your staff to support a policy that you either ignore or half-heartedly enforce.

And how well does your staff comply with your directives? Do you allow one individual to ignore them while expecting the rest of the staff to comply? Or do you have equal tolerance and justice for all? Once issued, it must either be complied with by

TYPICAL DUTY AND ASSIGNMENT BOARD

MONDAY	TUESDAY	WEDNESDAY	THURSDAY	FRIDAY
JOHN: Mail back all tapes	JOHN: Check all PA pgms for week			JOHN: Insure all weekend pgms are in control room
MARK: File all copy		MARK: File all copy		
ED: Collect all time cards		ED: Remote at Jones' Rest. at 3 PM		
RICH: Change gold records	RICH: Change gold records		RICH: Change gold records	RICH: Change record list
MACK: Tape Rev. Smith at 2 PM				

Note: With a Duty Board posted, it becomes the announcer's responsibility to check it when he arrives each day for any "write-in" assignments.

28

everyone or the directive must be publicly denounced. Never just let a directive die a natural death. If you instruct the staff to do a particular thing (such as coming out of the news in a certain manner) and fail to follow up to make sure your instructions are carried out, you may rest assured that most of your future directives will be partially if not entirely ignored. Remember, and you don't have to remind the staff, your actions will spell it out: You are the boss! And, sometimes, boss spelled backwards is double sob.

DELEGATION OF DUTIES

Another common mistake of young program directors (and many old program directors) is the failure to properly delegate responsibility. Today radio is too technical, too involved, too diversified for one man to be able to handle all the infinite details that need attention. Therefore, it is mandatory that a program director, to be successful, delegate duties and responsibilities. To me, the most effective program director is the fellow who sits behind his desk and delegates. He's the smart program director. He's getting the job done and he's doing what he's paid to do—manage a staff and a department.

Unfortunately, most program directors adopt the attitude that if the job is going to be done right, they better do it themselves. This may be great for getting the job done, but as a program director you are also a teacher and you can't teach anyone without letting them try their hand once in a while. The important thing, though, is that by not delegating duties and responsibilities, a program director ends up "spread too thin." Too many things to do in too little time. Consequently, performance and efficiency suffer.

Another point must be mentioned. Do not get in the position of being afraid of your staff. Quite often an aggressive member will put you in the position of being subconsciously fearful of your own job. That aggressive announcer becomes a threat and subconsciously (sometimes consciously) you are apt to stifle this man in order to make your own job more secure. On the contrary, encourage this aggressive man. He can only make you look good. A good manager is surrounded by sharp people. Futhermore, a little competition never hurt anyone. If you have one or more sharp people on your staff, this will serve to keep your adrenalin flowing and keep you on your toes. Personally, I always like to have at least one and preferably two or more on the staff who would like to have my job. So, delegate. Let them make you look good. And let them take credit for a good job. The manager will know who did the job, but, more importantly, he will also be aware of **who got the job done.**

ADVANCE PLANNING

Can you name three events scheduled to occur in your market within the next 30 days? If you could name more than three, you're in great shape. If you could name only one, that's not bad. However, if after all your concentration you couldn't come up with one local event for next month, you have a problem. Not knowing what is scheduled to happen in your community is to be considered a crime of the greatest magnitude in the programming department. And even worse is knowing what is scheduled and not making plans, in some manner, to reflect your knowledge or awareness over your radio station.

In today's very sophisticated world of radio, the station that does not reflect community awareness is going to be located at the very bottom of the stack in both ratings and sales. If your sales department is in any way successful, you can bet the sales manager and general manager do a lot of advance planning. It's the only way they can sell properly and effectively. **And it is the only way you can program your radio station.**

There is no secret involved or any shortcuts in advance planning. It takes a little work and a little research. To me it is the second most important ingredient in good programming. (The first ingredient will be discussed in the next chapter.) Advance planning gives you several opportunities to be creative—a vehicle for use as a promotion campaign, a public affairs or public service announcement campaign, and very often a sales campaign.

Years ago, a station could very effectively put a campaign together overnight. And in many cases you can still do this; that's the beauty of radio—flexibility. However, your chances for success in any campaign or endeavor are greatly increased with a carefully thought out, carefully produced program—in advance—rather than overnight over a bottle of happy water.

How do you find out what is happening in your market? May I first suggest that you obtain a copy of Chases' Calendar of Annual Events (Apple Tree Press, Box 1012, Flint, Michigan 48501). This little book is published every year by Mr. William D. Chase and is an invaluable programming tool. Mr. Chase compiles a list of events scheduled for an entire year. In this book, in order by the month, you'll learn when such little gems as National Pickle Month are scheduled. You'll find the dates that the Restaurant Association will observe National Restaurant Month. Everything from The League of Elderly Gentlemen Week to when the swallows are going to return to Capistrano. And many of the events are capable of being observed (even scheduled to be observed) in your market. A check with the local Chamber of Commerce will let you know if there is going to be any local participation in an event. And if there is no local participation planned, what's to prevent you from having your own promotional, public service, or sales campaign?

You will also want to start a "local event suspense file." Just a calendar, with all months visible at a glance, on which you make entries concerning upcoming events. Civic and business leaders generally announce several months in advance when they have decided on a particular campaign. If you watch your local paper, you'll get the date and be prepared for it. Many states publish a list of scheduled monthly events and I would suggest writing your state tourist director to obtain this list for your suspense file. And before we get off the subject, keep this in mind. Many station people belong to some sort of organization. And as such organizations plan upcoming events, get staff members into the habit of reporting to you. Make the station people your community club spies. Have them report on the meetings they attend.

The value of advance planning should be quite obvious. If an upcoming event has sales possibilities, you will have ample time to advise the sales department and they, in turn, will be able to plan a sales package geared around it. For example, if you notify the sales department at least 30 days in advance of National Restaurant Month, there is a pretty good chance they will be able to sell a spot campaign to the local restaurant association or at least to many of the individual restaurants. And, of course, if the upcoming event has promotional or contest possibilities, advance planning gives you time to procure your prizes, work out all the details, and produce all the spots necessary to make the campaign entertaining, exciting, and successful.

One thing I want to make clear! Advance planning means in advance. Check the month of April on the the first day of March. Allow yourself 30 days of thought and preparation. And by all means, submit a list of the next month's scheduled events to the manager and to the sales department. You may not see the potential commercial possibilities, but they might. It will be another feather in your cap. Let them know that you are on the ball. Advance planning! It has made great program directors out of mediocre ones. So, get on the bandwagon. Get your suspense file established and start some planning.

CONCLUSION

We'll ask the question again. What is a program director? Whatever he is, and whatever his duties, he is a part of the management team. And as part of the team it is his responsibility to know his craft. Do not wait for someone to tell you what to do. Take the initiative and assume the responsibilities as they present themselves. The more capable you become in your position, the more valuable you become to your organization.

On-the-Air Programming

3

I have learned from attending conventions, seminars, and talking to other program directors that if you get ten program directors into one room to discuss formats, you will come up with ten entirely different approaches. And all ten may be good—for that particular market. Of course, that is the key. You adapt the best available for your particular needs and market.

On the other hand, if you had ten program directors in one room, they might disagree on technique and approach, but I think you would find they would be in complete accord on one matter. No matter what your format, your music, or your station image, the most important ingredient is consistency. Consistency in everything you do. **This is the prime ingredient or factor in programming a radio station or building a station image—consistency.**

I could easily spend several chapters outlining successful formats and formulas from stations across the country, but would they do you any good in your market? What's working in Sacramento may be the kiss of death in Richmond, Virginia. A station in Burlington, Vermont, may be number one, but their modus operandi could spell doom for a station in Augusta, Georgia. The point, of course, is to take the best from the best and adapt it to your market.

However, I can give you one guaranteed formula or format for success. I wish I could take the credit for this brainchild, but I can't. It comes from a Westinghouse broadcasting executive (from a speech at the Miami "Storz" DJ Convention of years ago) and is called the 3-E Formula. If properly applied, you can't lose. The Three-E Formula—Energy, Enthusiasm, and E-magination—can be found in any successful operation. Look at, or I should say listen to, the good ones and you will be able to detect it. An elderly program director (he happens to be three months older than I) once made the statement: "Give me a staff of 18-year old disc jockeys and I'll take any market in the country. They've got the energy and enthusiasm and I will supply the 'E-magination.' More important, everything is new to them and their enthusiasm will be boundless—and contagious." The gentleman very definitely had a point.

Format may be roughly defined as the general form or arrangement of your programming. Once you have decided on your format be sure you and your entire staff understand what and why you are programming in a particular manner. Over the past few years, hundreds of stations have adopted formats purely because the "giant up the road" was doing it. Programming features have been added to a station's format "because it sounds uptown."

Here's an example. Within just the past few years, hundreds of stations have adopted the idea of using 20-20 news. Or in plain language, news programmed at 20 past and 20 before the hour. A program director, somewhere, heard it being done in Los Angeles and thought it sounded great or "uptown," so he adopted the news innovation for his station. Soon, hundreds of stations were featuring 20-20 news without the slightest idea why, other than it was different and it sounded good on the air. Most program directors thought it was scheduled at 20 past and 20 before to beat the other stations. They thought it was to enable the station to be into music while the competition was in their news. That would be a pretty good guess. However, let's just suppose that the program director in Los Angeles did a little market research and found that the majority of residents who were driving to work had to be at their destination by the hour or the half hour. Therefore, by scheduling the news in these drive periods at 20 past and 20 before, the station would be reaching more people—the commuters. So, we end up with the Los Angeles station programming their format to reach the maximum audience and the copy cats programming their station because an idea sounded good.

The point is, **know your market and your audience.** I know of stations that are not even aware of when their "drive" times are. Everyone automatically thinks of drive time as 7 AM-9 AM and 4 PM-6 PM. Yet, in several instances I've found a market's drive times to be unusual. There is a market in South Carolina whose drive time is 5:30 AM-8 AM and 2:30 PM-4:30 PM. I found, after a little research, that the entire town revolved around two large mills and that the entire town went to work, got up for school, or started the day at unusual times. For years, the station had not sold any spots in the 5:30 AM-6:30 AM or 2:30 PM-4:30 PM segments because they were selling "drive time" at other times. And they were programming the same way. **You have to know your market.**

Now, let's examine some of the format factors that contribute to the success of a radio station.

MUSIC CONTROL

Be consistent in what you play. If you are going to be a hit station, play the hits. If you're going to be a middle-of-the road station, play the MOR hits. If you're going to be a country music station, play country music. Nothing irritates me more than to hear a member of a staff apologize for what the station is doing. If you are not sold on what your station is programming and you are not proud of your station or product, move to another station and do your thing. You can't sell it if you don't believe in it.

First you must define your target audience and then select the music that will deliver them. And, as program director, some sort of control must be exercised in programming your music. For the sake of brevity, I am going to present only two music control systems or formats.

Target Audience Rotation System or TARS

The TARS method allows the disc jockey some freedom in what he plays, yet enough control is retained to maintain a consistency of sound. Notice that there are four categories of records; A, B, C and Gold on the chart. "A" records are the very biggest hits. For the sake of explanation let's just say

6AM - 9AM	9AM - 2PM	2PM - 6PM	6PM - 6AM
GOLD	GOLD	GOLD	A
A	A	A	B
B	B	B	C
GOLD	GOLD	GOLD	GOLD
A	A	A	A
B	B	B	B
C	GOLD	C	GOLD
A	B	GOLD	A
GOLD	C	A	C
A	GOLD	B	GOLD
B	A	C	A
GOLD	C	GOLD	B
A	GOLD	A	GOLD
B	A	B	B
C	B	C	C
GOLD	GOLD	A	A
REPEAT	REPEAT	REPEAT	REPEAT

Target Audience Rotation (TARS) Format.

they are records 1 through 10 (could be 1 through 12 or 15, etc.) on the popularity charts. "B" records are the middle hits, not popular enough to be really big, but popular enough to warrant air play. This group might be 11 through 20. "C" records are hits on their way up or on their way down and are ranked 21 through 40. Gold, of course, is a reprogrammable hit from out of the past.

With the TARS method your records are categorized as far as popularity is concerned. However, you must now categorize your records for demographic or specific audience appeal. For example, you do not want to program a strong "teen appeal" record during housewife time. And by the same token you do not want to program a strong "adult appeal" record in peak teen listening time. Or, perhaps, your format calls for hard rock or ethnic oriented music to be played only during specific times. Then you must establish sub-categories. And the most simple way to identify records for each category is the utilization of color codes. From any office supply you may obtain various size, self-adhesive color dots. For the sake of presentation let's use this color code system: Yellow: record may be played anytime (broad appeal), Red: may be played only in drive time (limited appeal but strong record), and Blue: may be played only at night (teen appeal only). By placing the A, B, or C on the color dot, one glance tells the disc jockey which category the record is in and the color of the dot tells him during what time period the record may or may not be played.

For this control system to work, you will need four record bins or compartments, one for each category (A, B, C, and Gold). When the records are placed in their respective bins, the DJ will begin his program with the first record in the bin (as designated by the format) and after he has played it, he will place the record at the rear of the bin. In other words, he will always play the first record in each category bin, **unless** the color dot denotes that the record cannot be played in that time period. He then will rotate that record(s) to the rear and select the next record.

Each disc jockey follows the format sequence in the column or time period he is on duty, and just continues to rotate the records as they are played. I might mention that the sequence shown in the illustration represents an actual format being used by a station. However, the sequence and rotation may not be adaptable in your market. Whatever your rotation, the key is **consistency**. In the sequence shown, the program director is trying to achieve a balance between records, with the accent on the new hits and the gold hits. The **consistent** overall image is **hits—hits—hits.**

Incidentally, the rotation sequence may begin at any time. However, a DJ generally begins an hour when the news ends, regardless of the time the news is scheduled. Remember this: You should program your musical strength at the point where news ends and music begins.

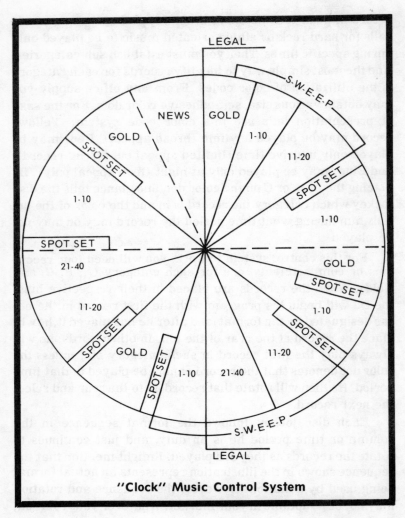

"Clock" Music Control System

Clock System

Another popular music control format is the "clock" system. The "clock" is still used in many stations, particularly in the smaller markets where managers demand more control of the music played by fledgling DJs. The illustration should be self-explanatory in that a particular record is played at a particular time. The clock diagram shown allows for two music sweeps and seven spot sets. Seven spot sets allow the DJ to get his commercial load in by clustering or piggy-backing the spots.

As with the previous control system, you may want to color code the records in the same manner to insure proper demographic programming. And you may want to establish a clock for each particular time period. I have known stations that used 24 different clocks, one for each hour of the day.

I could go into 30 different additional methods of controlling the music and I'm sure that I could get an argument for and against each one presented. Learn from other stations and program directors. Then develop your own system or at least devise the system that is best for your market, your station, and your personnel. The important thing is that you must have **consistency** and that is the reason for a format — to deliver consistency throughout every hour that the station is on the air.

MUSIC RESEARCH

This is a highly controversial subject. I know program directors who still "wing" it in making up their playlists and their stations are consistently number one in the ratings. I know still others who spend the greater part of each work week researching the sales of tapes, cassettes, cartridges, singles, and albums , and their stations are consistently number one. Common sense must prevail in this area. One thing is certain: You can't go wrong if you research your music each and every week. The important thing to bear in mind is not to spend so much time in music research that your regular programming duties suffer.

There are many methods of music research. The luckier stations have an "in" with the juke-box people and are able to correlate information obtained from juke-box play. Some program directors have the ability to get the information they want from the rack jobbers (perhaps the most important sales source), and still others rely solely on daily and weekly checks with the area record shops. I know of some program directors who rely entirely on the use of the telephone, conducting their own research, each day, with part-time help. Still others utilize the "DJ hotline." The jocks are provided a simple chart several days a week, and as they take calls they ask the listener several questions pertaining to music and music tastes. Other stations even use their secretary or receptionist. This little lady usually receives quite a few calls a day for requests (even though the station doesn't take them) and it's a very simple matter for her to jot down the record requested. Some stations even employ high school students and college students who serve on weekly panels and rate and prejudge new releases.

Years ago, music directors were content to know only how a record was selling. In today's programming it is important to know not only how well a record is selling but who is buying it and why. By determining **who** is buying a record, a music director is able to pinpoint the demographic appeal of a record, which then enables the program director to schedule the record in the appropriate time periods(s). It is important to know the **why** of a record's sales to insure that you are truly programming a record of listener appeal.

Some years ago, an album of questionable merit began selling rather spectacularly. Many stations began to program the album based on its huge sales success. It is natural for music directors to assume that if the public is buying a record, they want to hear it on the radio. However, one west coast programmer got a little curious, and after doing some very creditable research found that the record was being purchased, but the buyers would carry the record home and never listen to it. The album in question was a status symbol. It was "in" to have the record in a collection, but its appeal was almost nil. No one really wanted to hear the album, yet hundreds of stations programmed the album for several months— not even aware that they were programming a tune-out factor.

It is, as we said, important to know **who** is buying or requesting a record. We've all seen many instances of a hit or number one record which was purchased or requested only by teeny-boppers. Naturally, the demographic appeal of such a record is limited, in most cases, to teens only. So determine the demographic or audience appeal of a record before you program it. **Just because a record is a hit doesn't automatically mean that it should be programmed in all time periods.**

It is very important to know the ethnic appeal of a record. Any routine check with area record shops will show one record doing very well in one area, yet the same record is not moving in another area. Again, we go back to that important phrase—know your market. Some form of music research, for your market, is necessary. However, try to keep your methodology simple and easy.

AWARENESS

Your station is either aware or it isn't. You can't fake this factor or ingredient. Awareness comes only to those people who make it a full-time job and it takes on many forms. Awareness may refer to music, commercials, public service announcements, programming, news, and community activities. Awareness does not just happen. You have to make it happen. And without it, your station is just a run-of-the-mill operation. Therefore, it is very important that you know your community. Read your daily or weekly newspaper and check the Chamber of Commerce bulletins and memos. Let your station reflect the activities of your community. Let the listener know that you know what's going on.

Awareness means more than knowing what's happening in your community; it also involves what's happening on your radio station. Are your commercials being continually updated? How many times have you heard a station run a commercial which states: "Winter is just around the corner and it's almost time to get those snow tires on," while the outside temperature is 28 degrees and there is a foot of snow on the streets. Or have you heard a public service announcement which is plugging the Shriner's fish fry this Saturday, only Saturday was yesterday. Or a commercial which is broadcast at 7:30 in the evening urging you to shop "tonight till six." These little goofs make your station (and you) sound bush. It is suggested that any spot (commercial or otherwise) that is in any way dated by time or date have a stop time and date on the cartridge or copy. If your public service announcements or community bulletin board are read live, make sure that you have stop dates typed in on the card at the beginning of the copy. By typing the stop date at the beginning of the copy you will insure (almost) that the announcer does not get halfway through and then apologize lamely that the event has already occurred. Also, make sure that your record playlist reflects community awareness.

Everyone in the radio station should be aware of what is happening in the community. Be thankful that when a listener wants to know something, he automatically calls the radio station. If the person who answers the phone does not know what the listener desires, he should get into the habit of at least checking for the information. I never cease to be amazed by the number of station personnel who get irritated when a listener calls for a ball score, the weather, a concert schedule, or to find out what time the polls close. Even more unbelievable is the secretary or receptionist (and sometimes announcer) who can't advise a caller on a record or contest— that the station is broadcasting! Whoever answers the station telephone can make or break a station with that listener. Reflect awareness on the telephone as well as on the air. Make awareness your thing. Make your station alive and up-to-date in everything you do and say.

PUBLIC SERVICE ANNOUNCEMENTS AND PUBLIC AFFAIRS

I have always felt that a public service announcement or program should be treated with the same respect as a commercial. Oftentimes, in producing a commercial you are somewhat limited by the sponsor or client request in how you produce the commercial. You may find that your creative impulses are somewhat stifled. However, with public service announcements and programs, the sky is the limit on your creative ability. This is your opportunity to really show what you and the production department can do, and on many stations the PSAs and programs are real showcasers.

There's one important thing to remember. Most civic leaders are also the business leaders in the community. You have a great opportunity to impress them with your expertise with well-produced "commercials" for their clubs or organizations. Impress a person with what you can do with a public service announcement and he won't be so difficult to sell the next time a representative from the station calls to make a sales pitch. Make your announcements entertaining, informative, and imaginative. Treat your public affairs programs in the same manner. There's more on this subject in a later chapter.

QUALITY OF AIR SOUND

The greatest format in the world is utterly wasted if your station sound is sub-par. Let's first assume that your engineering department is doing the job and the signal is up to standards. When I refer to quality of sound, I refer to those areas which fall under the program director's responsibility. Are the jocks playing scratchy records? If so, replace them or don't play them at all. Particular attention should be placed on the gold records and big hit records because they get played the most often.

And how about your cartridges? Are they clear and clean, or do some have a muffled or bassy sound while others sound tinny? Replace them. Do the jocks start recording after the splice on the cart or do they record over the splice? If anything is recorded over the splice, the cart should be erased and re-recorded. What about your cartridge machine and tape machine heads? Are they cleaned regularly and systematically or just when they need it?

Are your intros and closes kept up-dated and fresh, or are you using the same ones from a year ago? Does your station sound flow or is it constantly interrupted by features such as weather, sports, bulletin boards, etc.? Keep the continuity of your sound. Your hour should be clean and smooth, with a minimum of interruptions. And most important, any mistake detected on the air should be corrected immediately. It's the small details that contribute to the quality of your air sound.

CONTROL OF JINGLES, PROMOTION SPOTS, PSAs, ETC.

Control of jingles is seldom a problem anymore. Most radio people have come to realize that a station jingle is not a spot separator; rather, it is an image builder. For all practical purposes, a jingle is either a music indicator (played immediately prior to a record) or a music associator (played immediately following a record). In establishing your format, determine where, when, and which jingle you want broadcast and set up a system accordingly.

Promotion spots and public service announcements are probably the least controlled features on a radio station. Many stations still broadcast these items on a "catch-as-catch-can" basis. Promotion spots and PSAs are generally placed in the control room, available to the disc jockey when they are needed, with virtually no assurance that each spot will receive adequate air exposure. The exception might be a promotion spot for a station contest and in this case the spot is deemed important enough to get scheduled on the program log. Any spot item placed in the control room should be scheduled on the log. Promotion spots are "commercials" for the station and public service announcements are "commercials" for civic clubs and organizations. By scheduling the spots on the log, there is a little more insurance that they will be broadcast.

If spots are placed in the control room and their broadcast frequency left to the discretion of the announcer, invariably each announcer will subconsciously have a favorite he will automatically reach for. Consequently, some announcements will get much more exposure than others. And if all the announcers "dig" one particular announcement, the station suddenly has a blitz going for one item. As an example, a national church organization produced a series of beautiful spot announcements built around the theme, "What Is Love?" You may recall the hit record by Tom Clay based on the announcements. At any rate, for months the majority of public service announcements aired by radio stations were these church spots. I'm sure the blitz had great impact because they certainly created comment. But what about all the other public service announcements that did not get aired because the disc jockey on duty had that discretion to play what he wanted. The most positive control of public service announcements and promotion spots is the station log. And it is also the only record of what was broadcast.

One other matter should be taken into consideration regarding the scheduling of promotion spots and public service announcements. The demographic appeal or target audience of each spot should be considered. Very few stations, for some reason, take this factor seriously. It just doesn't make much sense to broadcast a record hop promo at ten o'clock in the morning when the teens are in school and then turn around and broadcast a sewing circle meeting announcement at ten that night. **Remember, it is important to determine the target audience appeal of the spot and then schedule accordingly.**

FORMAT TYPES

Slowly but surely radio stations in almost every market have been moving in the direction of total specialization. That is, specialization with a particular type of programming in order to achieve maximum penetration within the station's desired target audience.

As I stated earlier, there are so many factors to be considered in programming a radio station. However, the prime factor is the station's "base carrier"—music or talk. A station is either one or the other (and as will be explained, occasionally a station can be a combination of both music and talk). Under these two headings are more clearly defined subcategories which immediately identify or define any given station's programming.

A **contemporary station** is usually referred to as a "Top 40" station. Many of today's modern radio concepts were developed by contemporary stations. And contrary to general opinion, the demographic appeal of this type station is not necessarily limited to teenagers. The spectrum may reach all the way from 12+ to 60 years of age. A contemporary station is "contemporary" or modern in sound, programming primarily the current hit records of the day.

A **middle-of-the-road** (M-O-R) **station** is theoretically exactly that: Programming in the middle of the road, not too far to the right and not too far to the left. Unfortunately, the term "M-O-R" is misleading. And many so called M-O-R stations resent the term. A more appropriate term might be the one used back in the late 50s, "chicken-rocker."

Chicken rock means that all the current hits are played, except those considered to be on the hard rock side. Years ago, stations did not play these particular records so as not to offend either the sponsor or the adult listeners. Hence, the term chicken rock. However, in today's M-O-R stations the harder sounds are omitted by design, not from fear. The programmers particularly omit "bubble-gum" or teen-oriented sounds and concentrate on records which have a broad adult appeal. M-O-R stations compete for the same audience, demographically, as the contemporary hit stations, and consequently, it is becoming more difficult every day to really tell the two apart.

A **country and western station** programs those sounds or records which are primarily associated with Nashville. You'll hear the station and its music format called many things: Countrypolitan, Uptown Country, The Nashville Sound, Blue Collar Soul, etc. But you will never hear any reference to "hillbilly" or "mountain music." C & W stations have become as sophisticated in their programming approach as their M-O-R and contemporary friends. Gone are the days of the "mouth full of grits down-home announcer." He's been replaced by a smooth and very knowledgeable professional. For years C & W stations were famous for their "station personality" (every country music DJ thought he was a personality if he took three minutes to deliver a 30-second commercial). Now, slick and professional production spots have replaced the live copy. Gone are the days of dead air, slurping coffee on the air, and "talkin' to them friends and neighbors."

Even today's music is much different. Only in the remote regions will you hear honest-to-goodness Bluegrass. Today's country music is almost borderline to being "pop." And in many cases country records actually cross the line into the pop field (i.e. Johnny Cash, Glen Campbell, Roy Clark, etc.) What has happened is that country music and country music stations have achieved respectability, due in part to the huge success of country entertainers in television and the change in outlook among station personnel.

The **easy listening station** should not be confused with the "background" station. Easy listening stations program only those records considered to be "easy on the ears." They often refer to themselves as the "adult" station. Programming is always low-key and somewhat on the subdued side.

The **background station** is also low-key, but even more so. There are no interruptions except for an occasional commercial or newscast. Vocal records are a rarity, since the accent is primarily on the instrumental selection.

The **progressive rock station** is just the opposite. While the interruptions may be kept at a minimum, the tempo or mood will vary from hour to hour, from selection to selection. The music, as indicated, is on the progressive side. And unfortunately, as of this writing, a stigma has been placed on some progressive rock stations. They are often thought to be the voice of all the "bearded weirdos" in the community. However, most progressive rock stations are "cleaning up their act."

Rhythm and blues station are most often referred to, inappropriately, as Negro stations. The music featured may be black-oriented, but many R & B stations are slowly finding that whites as well as blacks can be attracted to the R & B format. Just as the country stations grew up, so are the R & B stations. "Cool Daddy," "Sweet Lips," and "Mr. Groove" have become more sophisticated in their approach to their listeners. And station management has become more attuned to what an R & B station can accomplish.

The **ethnic station** is generally thought of as being the R & B station. I think this is a mistake. R & B music may be of ethnic nature, but the audience certainly isn't. I prefer to think of an ethnic station as one which programs primarily for a specific audience—in a foreign language; for example, a Spanish station or Italian station. The music is of an ethnic nature, generally, and the announcers speak the native tongue.

The **classical station** is just that. Classical music from sign-on to sign-off.

Block programming is a carry-over from the old days (pre-1955) when a station tried to be all things to all people. The title is exactly what it infers: programming or programs served up in blocks. There might be a 3-hour country music block, followed by a 2-hour good music block, followed by a swap shop, etc., etc. This type of station is still around, however, generally in the small markets. And although it might appear that a block-programmed station is violating all rules of programming, it is not. To begin with, a block-programmed station is consistent in what it does. And in everything it does, public service and information to the community is paramount. The station literally has something for everyone.

The **all-news station** offers nothing but news—all the time. No matter what hour of the day you dial an all-news station, you'll hear the news, commentary, or special reports. Due to economic factors, an all-news station is generally found only in the larger markets.

The **news and talk station**, also, features no music. The accent is on news and talk programs. The programs are either panel discussions, with experts from various fields, or audience participation programs in which listeners call the station (or program host) and present views and opinions.

The **news-talk-sports stations** add one other little ingredient: play-by-play accounts of sports events.

Have I left anyone out? Of course, there are many variations of the preceding categories. For example, a station might be M-O-R in the daytime and then switch to Top 40 at night. There are stations that play easy listening music all day and then program R & B all night. It all comes down to the fact that a station must determine its target audience and then program accordingly.

HOW TO DETERMINE A NEED AND HOW TO SCHEDULE.

Music is the "base carrier" or the prime program factor, unless the station is geared to a talk format, of course. Once the music (and control method) has been determined, then the programming subfactors or components must be considered. These components are, generally, referred to as features. Essentially, they are news programs, weather, sports, and any programmette of an informational nature such as stock market reports, beach conditions, school menus, etc. No one can advise you on what to program and at what time to program it. This information can be determined only after researching your market. However, several general suggestions might be helpful to you.

First, before you insert any feature into your programming structure you must determine if there is a need in the market for the feature. Far too many program directors insert features because (1) they, personally, relate with the feature, (2) the sales department wants to sell it, (3) the competition is doing it, (4) the station up the road is doing it, or (5) it sounds uptown. So determine if there is a need for the proposed feature in your market before inserting into your programming.

Second, is the information for the feature easily and economically accessible? The worst thing you can do after initiating a particular feature is to later be forced to discontinue it because it became too difficult or too expensive to obtain the necessary information.

Third, will the feature disrupt the flow of your format? Can the feature be kept brief so as not to interfere with the smooth, continuous flow of your music? (There are extenuating circumstances in connection with this question. Any community emergency could lengthen a feature yet retain valuable programming properties. For example, a snowstorm would result in lengthy school announcements or a hurricane would, of course, result in lengthy weather announcements. I mention this because I once had a program director fail to properly take advantage of such a situation because I had failed to properly advise him.)

Fourth, will the feature appeal to the station's target audience? Just because you determine through research that a need for a feature does exist, this does not necessarily mean that your station is justified in carrying a particular feature. For example, it would not be wise to carry the poultry market report when your station barely gets out of the city limits or there just aren't any poultry farmers in the city.

Fifth, will the feature enhance or detract from the station's overall image? Regardless of whether there is a need, how will the feature help or hurt the station?

Sixth, if all the answers to the first five questions are positive, what is the demographic appeal of the feature so that you may properly schedule the feature?

These are the six basic questions to consider before making any programming additions or deletions. **Never make an addition or deletion without first doing some thorough research on the matter.**

Now, let's look at some of the more common components and features and try to answer a few of the above questions, or at least attempt to show you how to answer to them.

News: The amount you have to carry has been predetermined in the station's committment to the FCC. Find out how much your station is supposed to carry and then start from there. If the figure is not high enough (this rarely happens), you may have to increase the news. If you have too much, you will need to start working immediately to get the percentages lowered by the owner at the next license renewal time.

Where should the news be scheduled? Only you can answer that question. Just because the station has always had news at :55 doesn't mean it has always been right. You will need to know these four things: (1) The shift times of the top industries or factories in the market; i.e., when do the workers begin and-or end their work shift, (2) The traffic flow in your city; this information may be obtained from the state highway department and the city traffic office. Ever see those insulated wires stretched across streets in your city? Chances are that the wire is connected to a counter which is counting the number of cars crossing that point in a given hour, day, week, or month. Bar graphs are then drawn, which reflect the flow of traffic at various points in the city. These graphs will indicate to you as a programmer the heaviest traffic situations and at what time of the day they occur. You will also need to contact (3) the schools to determine the start of classes each day, and (4) then determine at what time the office workers proceed to and from work.

From this information you will be able to determine (from the facts coupled with your own personal knowledge of the market) at what time you can best schedule your newscasts.

The above information will, of course, determine the best times for your drive-time newscasts, but I have always followed the policy of using the same times for the remaining part of the day (even though I appear to be contradicting myself by failing to research those times; your traffic graphs will bear you out on whether you're right or wrong in this assumption). **The availability of audience determines the time your newscast should be scheduled.** However, remember that, in many cases, news is a tune-out factor. So, always try to schedule your news in the **last five minutes of any quarter hour selected.** The reason is that the first ten minutes of that quarter hour are needed to establish your audience. Therefore, consider where your competition has the news, and if you can get the jump on them by five minutes without having your news on a quarter hour mark, by all means do so. I personally hold the attitude that I will go heads up with the competition. Many times you can't do it, though.

Something else to consider if you are a network affiliate: Do not hesitate to move the network's newscast (in drive-time) if your research warrants such a move. It might take a little doing, but with enough justification the network will in most cases allow you to delay the news or drop it altogether for a specific important time period.

When I first started in radio, the opening to the news was almost as long as the newscast itself. However, times have changed and today the less said at the beginning, the better off you are. Literally sneak into the news and, of course, avoid telegraphing the news (by DJ comment: "News is next and we'll be back on the other side," etc.).

Weather: There is some unknown inner force that compels radio people to feel that every weather forecast should be at least 30 seconds long and that it should be given after every record. There is that same compulsion to inform the listener after every record that skies are either cloudy or clear. The weather, obviously, has become a crutch for DJs and a sales tool for the sales department. Weather should be kept brief and to the point. And the complete forecast given an absolute minimum of times. No openings or closings are needed. Inject the weather into your program over the instrumental intros of records. Don't isolate it. Don't showcase it. Let the weather be a "subliminal" part of your programming. And keep it brief.

Sports: I am almost inclined to advise you to forget sports. I've always had a tendency to consider sports, in any form, as a tune-out factor on radio. And I am a dyed-in-the-wool sports fan. That is probably the reason. I lose my objectivity. I'll watch sports on television, watch it in person, and read the sports pages of the newspaper every morning without fail. Yet a sportscast or play-by-play account of an event leaves me cold unless, of course, it's a real biggie.

Those in radio who are sports minded have a tendency to give too much in a sports report and those who are not sports minded either give too little or too much of the wrong sport. I think, perhaps, the best policy in regard to sports reports is to limit them to one short one in the morning drive period and then another one in afternoon drive. Sports reports during the day should be limited to sports bulletins only. Again, a knowledge of your market and audience will determine what you should do in the way of sports. One thing to remember: You're in good shape by staying with the major and local sports stories.

Community service announcements: For many years, the policy in regard to community service announcements (local PSAs) has been to have a feature such as "The Community Bulletin Board," or "Community Calendar of Events." These features were broadcast each hour at a scheduled time, and the announcer would read anywhere from four to eight club announcements. Fortunately, this policy has changed and community service announcements now "float" throughout every hour. Or, in other words, each announcement is used as an individual item, rather than buried among other items in a time consuming "feature." Now, as it should be, the community service announcement is a controlled and regulated part of the DJs chatter and yet still remains a station feature. PSAs should be brief, to the point, and as I mentioned previously, scheduled according to the demographic appeal of the announcement.

However, if you decide to program a regular "bulletin board" type feature, you will certainly not be doing anything wrong. Be consistent and schedule the feature every hour and keep your material fresh and up-to-date. If it is to be a regular feature, avoid the long drawn-out opening and closing. Here it is, that's it, and then music. **Brevity.**

Time: Very simply put, the time should be given after every record without fail. The time is an image builder. When a listener thinks of the time, he should automatically think of your station.

Temperature: The temperature should be announced after every record. Just as the time helps to build your image, so does the temperature. The listener learns to expect to hear the temperature on your station. Therefore, when he really wants to know what the temperature is, your button is punched up. Mention the temperature after every record, in some form or manner.

Special Features

Lost dog announcements, when used as a special feature, have been called the "Dog-Gone Bulletin Board," "K-9 Roundup," "Pet Watch," "Dog Watch," etc. No matter what you call this feature, it can be one giant pain in the neck. The feature is great because you can earn some very loyal fans (by finding their pet), but if you carry this feature, resign yourself to phone call after phone call after phone call. You could eventually wind up carrying nothing but lost dog announcements. If you feel the station must carry lost pet announcements, I would suggest featuring the announcements on one program only. Assign one DJ to handle all pet announcements and caution him about getting carried away with lengthy descriptions and pleas to return the animal to the owner.

Fishing reports are, to me, an invitation to disaster. If you have fishing reports, **never** allow any member of the staff to give them. Always arrange to have someone at the source of the information record the report. It has been my experience that dock, pier, and boat operators are extremely optimistic when giving a fishing report. And it's easy to understand why. They want as many people using their facilities as possible. So they certainly aren't going to give a negative report. Therefore, it behooves the station to use the actual voice of the operator or source reporter on fishing reports. Irate listeners, who drove 50 miles and caught no fish, can then vent their wrath toward someone other than the radio station. If done properly, fishing reports make an excellent feature. Most stations air the reports Friday afternoon and Saturday morning. However, I would suggest that the reports be aired every day, particularly if the station is in a good fishing locale. Select a time between 6:30 AM and 9:00 AM and air a short, brief report every morning. This report will retain your avid fishermen listeners and serve also to excite the imagination of the once-a-year fishing buff.

Stock market reports are tune-out factors. Regardless of how much you've read about the public interest in stocks and bonds, that interest usually is nonexistent in radio programming. However, if there is a need and it is felt that the station should air the stock market reports, **keep the report brief**. If the report is to originate in a stock broker's office, advise the broker to keep the report as brief as possible and to give only items which have broad interest and appeal. You might also do a little quizzing of the brokers (I doubt if you get much information but you might). Ask them how many accounts the office handles. If you can obtain a rough estimate from each broker, you'll probably want to reconsider carrying the stock market reports. If you do carry them, the obvious place to schedule the report is in the afternoon after the exchange closes for the day. I always scheduled the stock market report in the last five minutes of the afternoon drive shift.

The PD's
Administrative Duties

4

Unfortunately, programming is not all music and promotion. There are certain administrative functions which require the PD's daily attention in order to maintain a smooth, error-free operation. Master these administrative areas because it is in the field of administration that you are really measured by your associates and your general manager. We suggest a system for each area covered; however, bear in mind that the particular system mentioned is meant to serve only as a guide. The best system is the system that works for you and your station. The important thing is that you do maintain a system.

PRODUCTION

The quickest way to incur the wrath of the sales department and your boss is to permit errors to occur in the production of commercials. Needless to say, you may be the greatest programmer in the country with a brilliant track record for ideas and innovations. But your genius will be forgotten if you can't get your department to correctly produce that which is requested by the sales department.

The following system is almost foolproof for handling production. Of course, there is still a margin for error, but the chances of a mistake are minimized considerably if the system is followed step by step. You may have to make a few adjustments for your particular situation.

First, you will need the following items for use in your production system: Large blackboard, large square of white poster paper, an equal size sheet of plastic, seven boxes or a rack with seven bins (for each day of the week), two file baskets, chalk, grease pencils, and Magic Marker(s). Mark off the blackboard in the manner shown at the top of

```
                        BLACKBOARD
   CLIENT    SPOT STARTS      ANNCR        CART No.
   ┌────────┬──────────────┬───────────┬───────────────┐
   │        │              │           │               │
   ├────────┼──────────────┼───────────┼───────────────┤
   │        │              │           │               │
   ├────────┼──────────────┼───────────┼───────────────┤
   │        │              │           │               │
   ├────────┼──────────────┼───────────┼───────────────┤
   │        │              │           │               │
   └────────┴──────────────┴───────────┴───────────────┘

               POSTER PAPER  CCB

   CART NO.          CLIENT              STOP DATE
   ┌────────┬──────────────────────┬───────────────────┐
   │   1    │                      │                   │
   ├────────┼──────────────────────┼───────────────────┤
   │   2    │                      │                   │
   ├────────┼──────────────────────┼───────────────────┤
   │   3    │                      │                   │
   ├────────┼──────────────────────┼───────────────────┤
   │   4    │                      │                   │
   ├────────┼──────────────────────┼───────────────────┤
   │   5    │                      │                   │
   ├────────┼──────────────────────┼───────────────────┤
   │   6    │                      │                   │
   └────────┴──────────────────────┴───────────────────┘
   ETC.
```

the accompanying illustration. On the large white poster paper (the cart control board), mark off divisions as shown in the illustration.

Post the blackboard and the cart control board in an obvious and convenient location and cover the cart control board (white poster paper) with the equal size plastic sheet so that client and stop date information may be entered with a grease pencil. Now, label one file basket "To Be Done" and the second file basket "To Be Filed." You are now ready to implement your production system.

Step 1. Salesman turns in the start order (in duplicate) and production order (copy information and instructions) to the traffic girl.

Step 2. Traffic girl goes to the cart control board and assigns a number to both the start order and the production order. At this point she has two steps: To enter the client name and stop date opposite the selected cartridge number and to enter the assigned cartridge number on the start orders and production order. She now gives one copy of the start order and the production order to the program director.

Step 3. Program director assigns the production to an announcer by writing the assignment on the blackboard, then places the production order in the "To Be Done" basket. (You may elect to have more than one file basket. You could have one for each man in production, then it could well serve as a mail basket or note and memo basket also.)

Step 4. When the announcer comes on duty for the start of his production shift, he checks the blackboard for assignments, pulls the production order from the "To Be Done" basket, writes the copy, produces the spot and records it on a cartridge, numbers the cart, and places the completed cart in the box for the day it starts on the air. (Remember you have seven bins or boxes for each of the seven days). Copy and production order are then stapled together and placed in the "To Be Filed" basket.

Step 5. DJ goes to blackboard and draws a line through the completed assignment.

Step 6. Sign on announcer puts the carts in service. When he arrives, he simply takes the carts from that day's bin.

The above system will work perfectly only if a production order is turned in for every copy change. The key to the system is that an account never has a permanent number (this is where goofs occur). When the copy changes, the cart number changes. Even if the spot is an update or only has a word to be changed, assign a new number. In the case of a movie spot that will say "Starting Tomorrow," "Starts Today," and "Now Playing," the best policy is three different numbers. Of course, the system is applicable only to those stations who put the cartridge numbers on the log.

Logging the numbers is the only way because it eliminates the possibility of airing the wrong commercial. The alphabetical system is the lazy way of doing it. If you are using

WXXX RADIO

COMMERCIAL START ORDER

CLIENT NAME _____   ADDRESS _____   DATE _____

BILLING ADDRESS _____

COOP NEEDED _____ AFFIDAVIT NEEDED _____ FIRST BROADCAST _____ LAST BROADCAST _____

LENGTH: 60 SECONDS _____ 30 SECONDS _____ 10 SECONDS _____ OTHER _____

	MONDAY	TUESDAY	WEDNESDAY	THURSDAY	FRIDAY	SATURDAY	SUNDAY
(AA)							
(A)							
(AA)							
(B)							
(C)							

SPECIAL INSTRUCTIONS:

TOTAL # SPOTS THIS ORDER _____

RATE PER SPOT _____

TOTAL CONTRACT _____

CLIENT SIGNATURE _____ DATE _____

SALESMAN _____ DATE _____

58

the alphabetical system (carts are in alphabetical order in the control room), I suggest you immediately discard this method and begin to number the commercials on your log. You will get a little static from the girl typing the log, but the additional insurance against having the wrong commercials aired is worth the extra time involved.

Periodically, the traffic girl will take her dead start orders to the cart control board and erase the client and stop date

```
                   P R O D U C T I O N
                        O R D E R

CLIENT NAME_____

ADDRESS_____PHONE_____

NUMBER OF SPOTS TO BE PRODUCED_____(ROTATE)(SEPARATE) LENGTH ____SECS

TYPE OF PRODUCTION: ____STRAIGHT _____TWO VOICED ____MULTI VOICE

                    ____MUSIC _____NO MUSIC _____HARD SELL

                    ____SOFT SELL _____HUMOROUS

SPECIAL INSTRUCTIONS:



ANNOUNCER TO BE ASSIGNED: _____

COPY INFORMATION IS (ATTACHED)(WILL BRING IN)(CALL CLIENT)

FINISHED PRODUCTION MUST BE APPROVED: ____YES ____NO



SALESMAN_____ ORDER STARTS: _____(DATE)


                              ASSIGNED CART NO.


                              #_____


UPON COMPLETION OF PRODUCTION PLACE CARTRIDGE IN:

    (CONTROL ROOM)  (DAILY BASKET)  (PD)  (SALES OFFICE)

                         ANNOUNCER INITIALS_____
```

information for that number. It is important that she, then, immediately pull those cartridges from the control room to insure that they do not get on the air by mistake.

Another important characteristic of this system is that if the spot goes on the blackboard, no one leaves that day until the spot is done. If a spot doesn't start for a week, don't put it on the blackboard. Eliminate the chance that the copy will be lost or misplaced. The board should be clean before the staff is allowed to leave for any day. The afternoon drive man is the logical double-check man.

LABELING CARTRIDGES

Just as you label your records with all the information possible, your commercial cartridges (all cartridges) should be handled in the same manner. Labels for commercials should contain the following information: Cartridge number, client name, length of spot, start date, stop date, and out cue. This is a lot of information to get on a label, but it will certainly make for a smoother operation. A finished commercial should have a label which looks like this:

	Jones Furniture		30 secs
No. 141	Starts 5-6	Ends 5-7	
			OC-"shop today"

I might also suggest that you assign a color to each jock. You can either obtain color-coded labels or plain white labels and then assign a Magic Marker to each jock. For example, Art: blue, John: red, Mark: green, Bob: black, Agency: brown, etc. By color coding the commercials, they are easier to program. You also avoid situations where a spot recorded by a DJ follows a live announcement made by him during his air shift. This color-code system is most effective if you cluster your commercials. You will have a much better air sound.

You will have some kinks to work out in this system, but as we said earlier, improve the system to work for your station. The important thing is to have a system to minimize production errors.

LABELING RECORDS

I am of the school that believes you can't have too much information on a record. Any information that might be of value to the disc jockey should be included on the record label. Information such as start and finish times of records, date record was released, date record hit number one, date you started playing the record, name of album record was taken from (if applicable), and any other information you might be able to include. A record label might look like this:

2:45	S-O/E-f	rel-4/71
"OUTCASTS"	No. 1-5/2/71	blue

Translated, 2:45 is the actual length of the record, S-O means record has a zero start (starts with vocal) and E-f indicates the record ends by fading, rel-4/71 tells us the record was released by the station (not the manufacturer) in April 1971, "OUTCASTS" is the name of the album the record was taken from, No. 1-5/2/71 indicates the record hit number one on 5/2/71, and blue tells the jock the target audience of the record. Such information is also invaluable when the record reappears as a golden record.

TAPE SAVE SYSTEM

When the sales department or your boss requests a previously programmed tape (program or commercial), you should be able to find it in a matter of seconds. Can you? You will be able to if you set up the following "tape save" system. The most simple method of holding tapes for possible future use is the alphabetical system. Merely file the tapes away in alphabetical order. However, if you do not have access to a large file cabinet, you may want to consider using the numerical filing system.

The numerical system is the most foolproof method of holding and finding tapes; however, it is also the most time consuming. It is based on a master card index. On a three-by-five file box, tape a card with numbers from one to as high as you can go on the card. As a tape is received, assign a number and mark that number off the master number sheet taped to the file card box. On another three-by-five card, type or write that number with the client's name and the client or agency reference number. You may also want to add the number of cuts and the subject content of each cut. Mark the assigned number and the client name on the outside of the tape box and file the tape away with the other tapes in numerical order. When that tape is requested, you simply go to the card index, look up the client name, find the card with the cuts you want and get the assigned number. You have the tape. As I said, this is the most time consuming method of saving tapes, but it is a good one.

If you receive a commercial on disc, make a tape recording of the disc and file the tape away. Especially if the commercial is a movie E.T. Theatre managers generally want the transcription returned after you have used it; therefore, it is a good idea to tape the commercial while the disc is in your hands. Plus, in almost all cases, that movie will be back for another run at one of the smaller theatres or at the drive-in and you'll have the commercial on file for use as a commercial or even a spec tape for your sales department. Save those commercials and have them filed in such a manner as to allow you to put your hands on them in a hurry.

COPY FILE SYSTEM

If your station employs a full-time copywriter, you don't have a problem. However, more and more of the smaller stations are dispensing with the services of a copywriter and utilizing the jocks to write and produce the desired copy. If this is the case, watch your filing system. Nothing is more embarrassing than for the general manager or sales department to look for a piece of copy and be unable to find it.

You will recall that under the production system we suggested a basket labeled "To Be Filed." This is the copy basket. It is suggested that you assign to one man the responsibility of filing the copy, rather than allowing each jock to file his own. With the responsibility delegated to just one individual, it is much easier to track down a mistake or goof. It is even a good idea to allow only one person to look for a piece of copy. The more hands you keep out of the copy files, the neater they will be. Also, make sure that every piece of copy has the writer's name and the date the copy was written and programmed.

When filing the copy, do not allow any "miscellaneous" copy folders. This is the easy way and eventually your "miscellaneous" folder will have more copy in it than the entire section and you will not be able to find anything. Every client or account should have its own individual folder. There are exceptions. Christmas copy, for example, might be filed in one folder for reference and use the following year.

PROGRAM LOG SYSTEM

If you lose just one log, I would bet you ten bucks that would be the very log that would be requested by an FCC inspector. It never fails. Therefore, you need a system to properly insure that each and every program log is saved.

The most efficient method is to have the preceding day's log left under your office door at the conclusion of every broadcast day. Immediately check the log for any discrepancies. If there are discrepancies or errors, have then corrected that day. Then retain the log in a safe spot until the end of the month. At the end of the month, double check to insure that all the logs for that month are accounted for. I would suggest that you not bundle the logs up until the tenth or fifteenth of the month because the bookkeeper may have to refer to the logs for billing purposes. However, once she has completed billing, file those logs in a safe place, tied up and labeled for future reference.

CORRESPONDENCE

Open every letter that comes to your desk. It may look like a piece of junk mail, then again it may be something important. I repeat, open every letter and examine it before you throw it in the trash can. I once lost out on a free trip to Europe because I thought an envelope contained an army public service announcement when it actually contained an invitation to be the guest of the Army on a public relations tour. If the letter does require action, handle it immediately. Agency requests for information, applications for employment, listener requests, etc., should all receive prompt attention. The efficiency of your organization—and you—is reflected in how promptly you reply to your correspondence.

INTEROFFICE MEMOS

You will need two file folders for interoffice memos, one for out-going and one for in-coming. Save every memo that you receive, no matter how insignificant it may seem at the time. Memos from the boss, from the sales department, from a staff member, and from anyone within the organization are your insurance against possible future controversy or misunderstanding. And when you receive an interoffice memo, respond immediately. If the action required will be delayed for some reason, explain the delay to the person who sent you the memo. I have always made it a policy to handle station memos in a priority manner to insure that my "efficiency" image would not be tarnished. You might consider establishing a similar policy. I would also like to recommend that you get into the habit of issuing directives, delegations, and assignments by memo. With a copy in your file, misunderstandings are kept at a minimum.

Station Community Involvement

5

Community involvement is important. Each station and all its personnel should strive for **total community involvement**, not only because of the obligation to the public but for a more practical and tangible reason. Ninety percent of the civic leaders in the community either make radio buys or influence the buys. Total community involvement affects sales. Involvement by the station creates a favorable image, opens up sales sources and revenue, and creates and increases the listening audience.

There are many case histories where radio advertising has been sold to a previously unimpressed client due to the results of an effective public service campaign conducted by a radio station. One example concerned a large mid-western tire dealer who, for years, believed radio reached only teenagers. The tire dealer resisted all sales efforts by the station sales department. It was learned, however, that the tire dealer was very active in a particular civic club. To make a long story short, the tire dealer eventually found himself publicity chairman of one of the civic club's projects. When he approached the radio station for a "few" plugs, the station went all out. Creative **commercials** (remember?) were produced and scheduled for maximum effect and the station even did a remote broadcast from the site of the civic club event on the day the event occurred. The results were almost unbelievable for the tire dealer. As publicity chairman, he was in a position to assess the publicity efforts of all the media and he became convinced that radio was primarily responsible for the huge success of the civic club event. Consequently, he became more receptive to the station's salesman and at this writing is one of the station's largest advertisers. All because a station became involved.

When you stop and think, radio really has a tremendous advantage over the newspaper and the television station. The television station is extremely limited in what it can do in promoting community projects. The available spot time is primarily reserved for commercial announcements and you probably have observed that the TV public service announcements which are scheduled are generally of national or regional interest. Local announcements are confined to a woman's program with just a token mention. The newspaper, on the other hand, thinks of a public service announcement as "dead news" once it has been printed. The newspaper does not often run an item more than once or twice on local activities.

Radio, though, is able to devote ample air time to any and almost all civic club projects and activities. And more importantly, perhaps, radio is able to be more creative in its approach and delivery than either newspaper or television.

It should be rather obvious that community involvement requires a great deal of planning, imagination, effort, and originality, but the rewards are great.

PUBLIC SERVICE ANNOUNCEMENTS

Remember when we used to log a record hop promo as a public service announcement? Or when we could fulfill our responsibilities by scheduling Navy announcements or Radio Free Europe spots? If a station's public service announcements now consist of only "canned" spots from national organizations, that station is in trouble and is not fulfilling its obligations to the public. Today, public service announcements are on an entirely different level, or should be. They should be locally oriented.

Of course, it is much easier to just use a national PSA. There is less time involved, and certainly, in many cases, the national PSA provides a welcome change in sound. However, the question must always be asked, "Is the national PSA relative to the market?" For example, is a "Keep America Beautiful" spot made by a well known TV personality as much in the public interest as a "Keep Our City Clean" announcement by the mayor, police chief, or garden club member? In the eyes of the FCC you get the same credit for a "Join The Navy" announcement as you do for a "Lion's Club Broom Sale" spot. However, which one would be more relative to the market? And how about that national organization which urges the listener to send money to help feed starving people halfway around the world when in your own market there are people subsisting on just barely enough to stay alive. Please do not interpret this to mean that a station should not broadcast national public service announcements. What I am trying to say is that the majority of PSAs should be of local origin because that is where the station's action is—**on the local scene.**

In Chapter 2 we mentioned the establishment of a local event suspense file. From this file a station should attempt to plan public service announcements at least 30 days in advance. The knowledge of an upcoming event allows the station to call or write the club or organization and offer the station's services in promoting the event. (It's a safe bet that neither the television station or newspaper will do this.) By contacting the club before they contact the station, it shows that the station is on the ball (awareness) and you will be amazed at how impressed the club members will be. I always tried to write the organization because I knew that the letter would be read into the minutes of the next meeting, thereby creating two image impressions; one, when the letter is read and then again when the minutes of the meeting are read at the following meeting.

Small and medium market stations have a distinct advantage over the larger markets in handling public service announcements. They are able to use "first-person" actualities or the voice of a club member to plug the event. This serves a dual purpose. One, in order to record the announcement, the member must come to the station, which enables the station personnel to do a little public relations work on a person-to-person basis. Secondly, when the announcement is aired, it's a pretty safe bet that the person who recorded it will be listening (maybe they never listened to the station before) and it's also a good bet that they'll find some means of letting their friends and neighbors know that they are on the radio. A station can build its image and audience with public service announcements.

Another good habit is to treat public service announcements, as we previously mentioned, as if they were commercials. Most stations simply log "PSA" and the disc jockey writes in what he runs. I firmly disagree with this method. You can't be assured that the spot will be broadcast and you will have no record of how many announcements were actually run, unless you go back and check every log. I would suggest that a regular commercial start and production order be utilized in handling PSAs. This will insure that the PSA is treated in a professional manner. And with the start order, a station has an immediate and permanent record of how many spots were broadcast. Many clubs receive points from their national chapters for announcements aired on radio stations and they may request this information after a campaign is completed, so beat them to the punch. When an event has run its course, drop a note to the club president advising him of how many announcements the station did broadcast in their behalf. Again, the letter will probably be read at the next meeting and the station will receive additional "image impressions"; the letter will also serve as a reminder to the group of what the station has done for them.

Remember to maintain your PSA count at the level it should be in accordance with the station's FCC commitment. Most stations are usually over. However, it is important to remember that if you are one hundred over every week, the FCC could care less. But if the station is just one short in the composite week, it's a "gig."

PUBLIC AFFAIRS PROGRAMS

I have never been convinced that most public affairs programs are not just a waste of time and effort. Maybe I am wrong and modern Americans spend 15 or 30 minutes glued to the radio, listening to a discussion on how to raise cabbages and cucumbers. I am more convinced that the public affairs and "other" categories of programming are not in keeping with the times as far as radio is concerned. And that the public interest would be far better served with a more rigid requirement on local community announcements. However, the Federal fellows say run them, so we run them. (Sometimes it appears as if the Commission will not be happy until all stations schedule only news and discussion programs.) At any rate, there is all the more reason to try and produce public affairs and "other" programs which are interesting and informative.

Consistently coming up with good PA and "other" programs could well be the biggest challenge a station faces each week. Most stations take the easy way and schedule syndicated programs such as Georgetown Forum, NASA Highlights, etc., which are available at no charge. I'm not saying these programs are not worthy of broadcast but they definitely are not of local origin and they do introduce a certain tune-out factor.

To begin with, in order for a program to qualify as a program, it must be of at least three minutes in length. And if the program is to overcome the tune-out factor it must be either timely or controversial, or both. Let's face it. If the program content deals with "raising hogs" or the "administrative problems encountered in managing a water plant," the listener appeal is going to be somewhat limited. However, a program dealing with the local drug issue or a confrontation and debate between two political candidates has a little more edge in retaining an audience. And the program doesn't have to run and run and run. A little editing will enable a station to cut a 30-minute interview into six or seven 3-minute programs. You still get the time credit and most of the tune-out factor is eliminated. So be creative and imaginative in your public affairs and "other" programming.

PROGRAM CLASSIFICATIONS

For your convenience and reference here is a list of familiar programs and how they are classified by the Federal Communications Commission (subject to change at any notice):

"Other" Category

University and college tapes

Live military news reports from local bases.

Job opportunity programs

Weather reports

All religious programs (live or taped)

Women's discussion programs

Political programs (not congressmen's reports)

Public Affairs Category

Georgetown Forum

Congressional reports (from area congressmen)

NASA series on space

Editorial

Health programs

Social Security programs

Tax tips

All local discussions, interviews, forums, and commentaries on local needs or problems.

Farm programs, farm price reports, sports, and community bulletin board announcements fall in neither category. Stock market reports are classified as news. If there is any question concerning the classification of a particular program, obtain an opinion from the station lawyer.

PERSONAL AND PERSONNEL INVOLVEMENT IN THE COMMUNITY

The importance of community involvement cannot be over stressed. It is essential that not only the station be involved but station personnel as well, no matter what that involvement is and at what level. **Involvement equals meeting people equals listeners and image.** It is as simple as that.

How does an individual go about getting involved? The quickest way is to join a local civic club. Quite a few stations now ante up the dues for any station employee who wants to join a local organization. If your station does not offer this policy, bring the idea up for discussion at the next staff meeting. It's just good business to have as many people as possible in local clubs and organizations. The contacts made are invaluable and the contributions one is able to make toward the community are immeasurable. However, due to the large turnover in personnel at the disc jockey level, it may be a little disadvantageous for a station to sponsor a club membership for every DJ on the staff.

However, DJs can get very involved in other areas. The Boy Scouts, Boys Club, Little League Baseball, and many other activities offer excellent opportunities for involvement by station personnel. I do not necessarily suggest an individual join an organization just for the sake of joining, but by being a member of a community organization the individual then becomes more aware of the community's problems and needs. And as a broadcaster, the individual is better equipped to reflect those needs on the air.

There is one pitfall to watch for. As a member of the station staff, publicity chairmanships naturally tend to fall in that direction. I've known instances where an overeager announcer would literally give the station away every time his club needed publicity for a particular project. And in this instance the club was the Jaycees, who have a project going 52 weeks of the year. Until the situation was corrected, the station sounded as if it was the voice of the local Jaycee chapter. When a staff member becomes a publicist for a civic organization, he must keep his enthusiasm in check. But be involved. The importance of community involvement cannot be overlooked.

6 | Commercial Creativity

What is a radio commercial? To me, it is a group of words designed to motivate an individual into a state of action. A commercial sells a product or idea to someone.

Unfortunately, a radio commercial has to compete with thousands of other commercial messages every day. Commercials, in some form or another, assault the public from every conceivable source. And even though there is some sort of commercial message almost everywhere, more than 80 percent of all advertising impressions are ignored completely. Ignored, primarily, because the public has more or less conditioned itself to tune out the commercial.

Then, how do you get the public to tune in your commercial? Very simply, the answer is creativity. And that is what we're concerned with—a creative approach to commercial production. We make no attempt to get involved in the psychology of copywriting. And there will be no attempt to convince you that the ideas set forth are the right way to produce commercials. There is no "right way." There is a right approach and that is what we are concerned with, the right way to produce a creative commercial.

Before anyone can sit down to the typewriter and begin to knock out masterpieces of commercial copy, he first has to know and understand the classifications of commercials. Ever wondered how many ways you can produce a commercial? The answer would have to be infinite. However, there are really 16 basic commercials or classifications. Familiarity with these 16 classifications is the first step of the "right approach."

STRAIGHT COMMERCIAL

The "straight" commercial is factual, to the point, and has no window dressing, other than perhaps a musical background. Here is an example:

ANNCR: LADIES, LET'S TALK ABOUT YOUR CLOTHES. OR BETTER YET, LET'S TALK ABOUT THE CLOTHES THAT ARE WAITING FOR YOU AT THE JULIANA DRESS SHOP, CORNER OF FIFTH AND MAIN. JULIANA, A TRUSTED NAME IN WOMEN'S APPAREL IN THIS PART OF THE COUNTRY FOR OVER FIFTY YEARS. TRUSTED, BECAUSE WOMEN KNOW THAT WHEN THE JULIANA SHOP AN-NOUNCES A SALE, IT'S REALLY A SALE. AND THAT'S WHAT THE JULIANA SHOP HAS NOW. A SALE THAT GETS UNDERWAY THIS WEEK. LADIES' BLOUSES AND SKIRTS HAVE BEEN REDUCED UP TO FIFTY PER CENT. SUITS AND COATS FOR FALL AND WINTER HAVE BEEN REDUCED AS MUCH AS THIRTY PERCENT AND YOU'LL FIND JUST THE COCKTAIL DRESS YOU'VE BEEN LOOKING FOR ON THE SPECIAL RACK OF EVENING WEAR FOR LADIES. ALL THE ACCESSORIES YOU NEED TO HAVE THAT WELL GROOMED APPEARANCE ARE AVAILABLE ALSO—AT GREAT REDUCTIONS. MAKE PLANS NOW TO VISIT THE JULIANA SHOP THIS WEEK. SHOP OR JUST BROWSE. THE JULIANA SHOP, CORNER OF FIFTH AND MAIN, DOWNTOWN.

PRODUCT DEMONSTRATION

The product demonstration commercial category generally includes situation type commercials with two or more people. The characters discuss the product or client's place of business. This category is most effective for driving home more than one thought or sales message.

SE: SAWING, HAMMERING, ETC.

1ST: HEY, CHARLIE. WHAT YOU DOING?

2ND: I'M TRYING TO FIX THE GARAGE DOOR. GLADYS DID IT AGAIN. DROVE THE CAR RIGHT INTO IT.

1ST: SHE AIN'T EXACTLY THE WORLD'S BEST DRIVER. BUT I'LL SAY THIS, CHARLIE. SHE IS THE WORLD'S BEST DRESSER. HOW CAN YOU AFFORD TO KEEP HER IN CLOTHES.

2ND: NO PROBLEM, SAM. SHE BUYS ALL HER CLOTHES AT THE JULIANA SHOP.

1ST: JULIANA SHOP? MY WIFE GOES THERE ONCE IN A WHILE.

2ND: WELL, THE ONLY PLACE SHE OUGHT TO GO. SAVE YOU SOME REAL MONEY, SAM. ESPECIALLY WHEN THEY HAVE A SALE.

1ST: SALES DON'T SAVE ME THAT MUCH MONEY, OL BUDDY.

2ND: THEY DO AT THE JULIANA SHOP. WHEN THEY HAVE A SALE, IT'S REALLY A SALE.

1ST: YEAH, BUT WHAT DO THEY PUT ON SALE. CLOTHES NOBODY WANTS.

2ND: NO, SAM. IT'S ALL BRAND NAME MERCHANDISE. THE JULIANA SHOP CARRIES ONLY THE BEST.

1ST: WELL, THESE SALES ALWAYS OCCUR WHEN I'M SHORT OF BREAD.

2ND: WHO NEEDS MONEY AT THE JULIANA SHOP. JUST CHARGE IT. TAKES ABOUT THREE MINUTES TO OPEN AN ACCOUNT.

1ST: I'LL DO IT. TELL MY WIFE TO OPEN AN ACCOUNT AT THE JULIANA SHOP.

2ND: GOOD. WE'LL HAVE THE BEST DRESSED WIVES ON THE BLOCK. NOW IF I COULD ONLY FIND GLADYS A GOOD DRIVING INSTRUCTOR....

In the product demonstration commercial, several themes or ideas are established: We said (1) that the best dressed women have clothes from the Juliana Shop; (2) that when the Juliana Shop has a sale, it really is a sale; (3) that they carry only brand name merchandise; (4) that it's easy to open a charge account; and (5) a subtle hint that husbands don't mind their wives buying clothes if they'll look sharp and save them money.

SITUATION COMMERCIAL

The situation commercial establishes an unusual situation between two or more people to drive home your message. As an example, refer to the Pepto Bismol commercial or the great Alka Seltzer commercials. These commercials vividly create a familiar situation and solve the problem with their product.

RIDICULOUS SITUATION

In a ridiculous situation commercial you establish a situation in which you drive home your message:

SE: CROWD AND TRAFFIC NOISE—STREET SCENE

GIRL: MISTER, ARE YOU FOLLOWING ME?
MAN: YES, BUT I CAN'T HELP MYSELF. YOUR CLOTHES ARE JUST ABSOLUTELY GROOVY.
GIRL: I COULD CALL A POLICEMAN, YOU KNOW.
MAN: TELL ME DEAR, WHERE DO YOU SHOP? LET ME LOOK AT YOUR LABEL.
GIRL: GET YOUR HANDS OFF ME.
MAN: JULIANA SHOP, OF COURSE. IT WOULD BE.
GIRL: LISTEN, IT'S GETTING SO A GOOD LOOKING GIRL LIKE MYSELF CAN'T WALK ALONE SAFELY ON THE STREETS ANYMORE.
MAN: LADY, IT'S THE JULIANA SHOP THAT SENDS ME.
GIRL: I DECLARE, MEN LIKE YOU SHOULD BE BEHIND BARS.
MAN: HEY, THAT'S NOT A BAD IDEA. LET'S TRY THAT ONE ON THE CORNER.

SE: MUSIC—UP AND UNDER FOR:

ANNCR: THE WELL DRESSED WOMAN GENERALLY

HAS CLOTHES FROM THE JULIANA SHOP, CORNER OF FIFTH AND MAIN, DOWNTOWN.

We could make this commercial even more ridiculous by changing the characters. Let the man take the girl's place and her take his.

FAKE CUSTOMER INTERVIEW

The fake customer interview is somewhat overused, but still effective with a little humor added.

SE: TRAFFIC NOISE—CARS—STREET SCENE

ANNCR: WE'RE STANDING IN FRONT OF THE JULIANA SHOP, CORNER OF FIFTH AND MAIN FOR ANOTHER MAN ON THE STREET INTERVIEW. AH, HERE COMES A SWEET LITTLE OLD LADY. EXCUSE ME, SWEET LITTLE OLD LADY...
LADY: YES, I AM.
ANNCR: I'M DOING A MAN ON THE STREET IN-TERVIEW. THE QUESTION FOR TODAY IS...
LADY: PARDON ME, SONNY, WOULD YOU MIND HOLDING THESE PACKAGES WHILE WE TALK. THEY'RE SO HEAVY.
ANNCR: YES, OF COURSE. NOW WHAT DO YOU THINK OF PEOPLE WHO WEAR MINI SKIRTS?
LADY: THINK OF THEM. I AM ONE OF THEM. WHAT DO YOU THINK I'M WEARING, SONNY BOY.
ANNCR: YES, OF COURSE. AND I SEE YOU'RE CARRYING LOVE BEADS. WHAT ARE YOU DOING WITH THEM.
LADY: OH, I BUY THEM FOR MY GRANDCHILDREN, SONNY. WELL, TIME TO RUN. BE A DEAR AND HELP LOAD THESE PACKAGES INTO MY CAR.
ANNCR: THIS IS YOUR CAR?
LADY: SURE IS. LIKE IT.

SE: SOUND OF SOUPED UP MOTOR REVVING UP AND DIGGING OUT

LADY: SOUPED IT UP MYSELF.

ANNCR: WELL, IF YOU'RE A DAUGHTER OR A GRANDAUGHTER, THE JULIANA SHOP HAS A DEPARTMENT FOR YOU. AND IF GRANDMA IS A SWINGER, WE CAN TAKE CARE OF HER TOO. THE JULIANA SHOP, CLOTHES FOR EVERY LADY...OF EVERY AGE.

REAL CUSTOMER INTERVIEW

The real customer interview also has been somewhat over-used, but such commercials can be extremely effective if done in the right manner. The proper way to utilize this category is to go to the client's place of business and obtain as many short interviews as possible. Do not make the mistake of trying to use the interview as it is recorded. Edit the interview, selecting short and believable segments for use within the spot.

SIXTH DIMENSION COMMERCIAL

The sixth dimension commercial uses the premise of shrinking time. We condense a long period of time into 60 seconds.

SE: MUSIC INTRO

1ST: JUNE 2ND, 1919, MISS SHERRY LEE WILSON WAS BORN. HER FIRST GIFT WAS A BEAUTIFUL PINK GOWN AND BLANKET FROM THE JULIANA SHOP.

SE: PUNCTUATOR

2ND: JUNE 2ND, 1920: MISS SHERRY WILSON RECEIVED ON HER FIRST BIRTHDAY HER FIRST LITTLE DRESS. IT CAME FROM THE JULIANA SHOP.

SE: PUNCTUATOR

1ST: SEPTEMBER, 1925. FIRST DAY OF SCHOOL FOR SHERRY. HER SCHOOL DRESS CAME FROM THE JULIANA SHOP.

SE: PUNCTUATOR

2ND: JUNE, 1937. SHERRY GRADUATED FROM HIGH SCHOOL. HER FORMAL CAME FROM THE JULIANA SHOP.

SE: PUNCTUATOR

1ST: APRIL, 1940. SHERRY LEE WILSON BECAME SHERRY LEE JOHNSON. HER WEDDING DRESS CAME FROM THE JULIANA SHOP.

SE: PUNCTUATOR

2ND: SEPTEMBER, 1942. SHERRY JOHNSON BOUGHT HER FIRST MATERNITY DRESS. IT CAME FROM THE JULIANA SHOP.

SE: PUNCTUATOR

1ST: JANUARY, 1962. SHERRY JOHNSON BECAME A MOTHER-IN-LAW. HER WEDDING RECEPTION ENSEMBLE CAME FROM THE JULIANA SHOP.

SE: PUNCTUATOR

2ND: MAY, 1969. SHERRY JOHNSON AND HER HUSBAND LEFT FOR EUROPE. HER BASIC WARDROBE FOR THE TRIP CAME FROM THE JULIANA SHOP.

SE: PUNCTUATOR

ANNCR: THE JULIANA SHOP. FOR OVER FIFTY YEARS, CLOTHES FOR EVERY WOMAN...OF EVERY AGE.

PUNCH-LINE COMMERCIAL

Many other categories occasionally rely on the punch line, but this particular grouping builds a story line or situation that finally reaches a climax or punchline. This is a clever type, but unfortunately this particular commercial gets old in a hurry. If you are going to tackle the punch-line variety, I would suggest several or more cuts. This will at least minimize the staleness over a period of time.

AUDIO PICTURE COMMERCIAL

The audio picture commercial uses sound effects with an idea to reinforce a thought or theme. The most familiar example of this type is the famous Stan Freeberg commercial. Remember the lake of chocolate, the airplane, and the maraschino cherry? The audio picture!

SE: THUNDER AND RAIN— ESTABLISH AND CARRY THROUGH ENTIRE SPOT

GIRL (SOFT, SLOW VOICE): WHEN I WALK IN THE RAIN, I WONDER ABOUT THINGS. LIKE AM I GOING ANYWHERE. IN MY JOB...MY CAREER, MY LIFE.

SE: FADE MUSIC UNDER VERY SOFTLY—LOVE IS BLUE

GIRL: MAYBE I WORRY TOO MUCH. I CAN'T CHANGE THE WORLD. BUT I DON'T WANT THE WORLD TO CHANGE ME. BEING A PERSON, THAT'S WHAT MATTERS. BUT I WORRY ABOUT THINGS. THE WAY I LOOK. THE WAY I DRESS. HAVING SOMEBODY THAT CARES. OH, THERE ARE SO MANY THINGS I WONDER ABOUT.....WHEN I WALK IN THE RAIN.

ANNCR: THE JULIANA SHOP CAN'T SOLVE ALL YOUR PROBLEMS. BUT WE DO HAVE THE ANSWER TO ONE OF THEM. WE CAN SHOW YOU WHAT TO WEAR....WHEN YOU WALK IN THE RAIN.

SPONSOR VOICE IMAGE

The sponsor voice image commercial actually uses the voice of the store manager or client to sell his own product and is particularly effective with clients who have egos or with clients who do not believe in radio. Let the one who doesn't believe in radio have just one person tell him they heard his voice on the radio and presto! A believer. You may have to do a little editing in order to make the commercial sound smooth, but whatever the work involved, it will be worth it. You'll have a happy client.

SPONSOR INTERVIEW

Very closely related to the sponsor voice image commercial is the sponsor interview. This type of commercial is rather time consuming in production but it can make a very happy and satisfied sponsor. Just as you do in the customer interview commercial, interview the sponsor, then go back to the studio to do some editing and building.

ELECTRONIC SOUND

The electronic sound commercial utilizes electronic music to produce effects or a mood for selling a product. The music builds the image of a "happening" or it gives the commercial a more contemporary flavor.

HISTORICAL FANTASY

The historical fantasy commercial utilizes a historical event for a base to sell the product or image. Of course, you generally have a prestigious historical individual involved:

1ST: I'D LIKE TO BORROW FIFTEEN MILLION DOLLARS.
2ND: I SEE. NAME PLEASE?
1ST: JEFFERSON. THOMAS JEFFERSON.

2ND: UH UH. IS THAT WITH TWO Fs, MR. JEF-FERSON?

1ST: YEP.

2ND: ALL RIGHT. OCCUPATION?

1ST: PRESIDENT OF THE UNITED STATES.

2ND: OF AMERICA?

1ST: DARN TOOTIN.

2ND: AND WHAT'D YOU DO BEFORE THAT, SIR?

1ST: WELL, UH.....I WAS IN THE REVOLUTION FOR A WHILE.

2ND: OUR SIDE?

1ST: UMMM UMMM

2ND: GOOD. NOW WHY DO YOU WANT TO BORROW FIFTEEN MILLION DOLLARS.

1ST: WELL, I'D LIKE TO BUY THE LOUISIANA TERRITORY.

2ND: YES...

1ST: NAPOLEON IS HAVING A SALE.

2ND: WELL, DO YOU HAVE ANY COLLATERAL?

1ST: HOW ABOUT NEW JERSEY?

2ND: ALL RIGHT. BUT THERE'S ONE PROBLEM.

1ST: WHAT'S THAT?

2ND: WELL, FIFTEEN MILLION DOLLARS FOR LOUISIANA. ISN'T THAT A LITTLE STEEP?

1ST: WHAT DO YOU MEAN?

2ND: WELL, I REMEMBER WHEN IT ONLY COST US TWENTY FOUR DOLLARS TO GET NEW YORK.

1ST: FRESH KID.

ANNCR: IF YOU NEED THE MONEY AND ITS FOR A GOOD PURPOSE, YOU'LL GET IT AT THE MAIN STREET NATIONAL BANK.

2ND: I WONDER IF YOU COULD GET THEM TO THROW IN CALIFORNIA.

IMAGE TRANSFER

The image transfer commercial uses the same theme or idea which is featured for a client on TV, billboards, or in the newspaper. Radio takes the same theme and adapts it for the audio medium only. A good example is a case where the idea used in a national TV campaign for an automobile is adopted for a local automobile agency promotion. The image transfer allows the client to capitalize on the national TV exposure in your market.

"QUICKIE" COMMERCIAL

I would rather have to produce ten 60-second commercials than just one "quickie." What can you do in 10 or 15 seconds? Well, it's hard, but it can be done. In the following, the client's image or product is effectively projected:

1ST: I MANAGED TO SAVE ONE HUNDRED DOLLARS THIS YEAR.
2ND: THAT'S NOTHING. I JUST SAVED ONE HUNDRED DOLLARS IN FIFTEEN MINUTES.
1ST: HOW DID YOU DO THAT?
2ND: FINANCED MY CAR AT MAIN STREET NATIONAL BANK.

"HOT" PROPERTY COMMERCIAL

It would be more appropriate to call this commercial the "what's in" commercial. This type utilizes a current popular phrase, program or fad. For example, when Laugh-in burst on the television scene, every station in the country capitalized on the various characters featured on the program. Another example would be commercials tied in with space shots. The "hot property" commercial.

IMPROVISATION COMMERCIAL

We said earlier there were sixteen basic commercials, yet there is a seventeenth which can easily be applied to all sixteen categories: the improvisation commercial. This type, to me, is the most enjoyable to produce. You utilize two or more members of the staff who sit down in the studio and carry on a conversation. You first establish a theme or general idea and then take off. The staff members just say what comes to mind and you record everything. After several conversations, audition the tape, and lift the usable parts. The segments selected should enable you to build or create a very interesting and effective commercial.

And there you have them—the basic commercial classifications. Familiarity with these classifications will enable you to at least approach your copy information in a creative manner. Select your category and then proceed to write and produce your commercial.

There are a few basic rules to bear in mind when writing a commercial. First of all, try to present your commercial in a new way or with a new twist. Don't begin with dull, unimaginative statements; instead open with a statement which will attract the listener's attention. Your commercial must be either natural and believable or so grossly exaggerated as to force the listener to retain the message. Remember, you cannot force the listener to focus his attention on your commercial. You can, however, make him want to listen. A commercial should invite the listener to participate. The listener should become so involved that he will actually provide or realize his own product benefits. In other words, the listener will sell himself.

Secondly, keep your commercial simple and your idea short. A commercial message is not the time or place for complicated, confusing, and complex ideas or thoughts. Keep the commercial message sharp, clear, and uncluttered.

Thirdly, always use "good voices" in your commercials. I have heard many potentially good commercials ruined with the use of a nasal-toned secretary (or girl friend) or someone from the sales department. I would suggest that you contact the little theatre organization or college and high school drama classes and literally hold auditions to find additional voices for use in your commercial productions. You can either pay them in albums or money. You'll find that generally they will be very enthusiastic about helping you and your commercials will sound 100 percent better.

Fourth, and possibly the most important, be sure that your finished product is technically perfect. Many great commercials have lost a little something with a bad splice, an overmodulated voice insert, or the wrong music. If you can detect one small mistake, by all means, do it over. The commercials you broadcast are reflections of your station's integrity. The sponsor is paying for that commercial and he deserves to get the best you have to offer. You owe it to him and to yourself to deliver the very best. Remember this: As we have mentioned before, a commercial is not to be treated lightly. It is your bread and butter.

THE FUNNY COMMERCIAL

Humor in commercials can be great. Too much humor, or ill-timed humor, can be devastating both to the station and to the client. When attempting to produce a funny commercial, make sure that the humor involved has something to contribute to the sale. The sale always comes first and humor second. The best example of this approach would have to be the Excedrin Headache commercials of a few years ago. They were beautifully produced, funny, and even today we have product retention in the form of Headache Number 29 jokes. However, the commercials sold very little Excedrin and were eventually replaced. Why? Because when you get a headache you think of anything but humor. The humor in a commercial has to relate to the product in a positive manner.

The most effective "funny" commercials are those which never, never make fun of the people who use the product; they make fun of the product. A perfect example is Volkswagen. What other company would dare call their product a lemon? In contrast, take the marshmallow meatball commercials for Alka Seltzer. They were wild commercials. But you'll notice they aren't on any more. And possibly because somebody suddenly remembered the cardinal rule: "You don't make fun of the people using your product." Who wants to relate to a dumb jerk who marries a broad who cooks marshmallow meatballs? And having a stomach ache is no laughing matter. So, if you are going to use humor, let the humor relate to the product in a positive manner.

WHERE DO COMMERCIAL IDEAS COME FROM?

Ideas come from every imaginable source. They come from monitoring other stations while you're driving in your car. They come from magazines, television, newspapers, handbills, billboards, the secretary, the sales department, and you. In other words, don't overlook any bet. And particularly do not overlook the advantages of being a member of the Radio Advertising Bureau (RAB).

I have never been able to understand why every radio station in the country doesn't belong to RAB. It is the only organization that is devoted solely to the radio industry. Of particular interest is the RAB commercial library and service departments. RAB not only provides you with sample commercial ideas (proven ideas from member stations) each month, but they maintain a permanent library of commercials for every conceivable type business. And member stations may borrow these commercials at any time at no extra charge or cost.

To be more specific, let's say that your sales department needs a new idea for a florist. A short note to RAB requesting some sample commercials dealing with the florist industry will get you a full tape of florist shop commercials by return mail. Then you merely sit down, listen to the tape, select the idea you like, adapt to your own client, and then return the tape to RAB. By being a member of the RAB, you have hundreds of copy writers creating ideas for you and your station all the time. If your station is not a member of RAB, I would suggest you do a little selling to the station manager. The cost per year, compared to what the sales department can realize utilizing their services is negligible. To contact the RAB, write 555 Madison Ave., New York, N.Y. 10022.

FILE YOUR GOOD COMMERCIALS

Once you obtain a good commercial, keep a copy in your own personal file. This file will serve you well as you progress in your career. In fact, the file will help your career. A good program director will always be in demand. However, if you are not only a good program director but can evidence a flair for commercial production, the sky is the limit.

ONE FINAL THOUGHT

Everyone in radio considers himself to be an excellent judge of what is good and what is bad in a commercial. From time to time you will be faced with a situation in which, perhaps, your best effort is turned down or torn apart by either the salesman or the sponsor. **Do not get upset.** And don't make an issue of it. Of course, be strong in your convictions, but not to the point where an argument over what is right or wrong with the commercial will strain relations between you and whoever is involved. Be charitable and relent. I've seen too many fine commercial production men never get anywhere because they wore their feelings on their sleeve. If you feel you have a good commercial idea and either the salesman or client disapprove, save the idea for use at a later date and give them what they think they want. Or better yet, accept the challenge —give them another idea.

Station Promotion  7

I think it is rather ironic that the radio industry preaches from day to day, "It pays to advertise," yet there are literally hundreds of stations which have absolutely no promotional or advertising budget set aside for use each month to promote or advertise its own product. And there are even more stations who do promote, but limit their promotional efforts to the radio media entirely, thereby contradicting another radio sales pitch, "It is necessary to reinforce any advertising campaign with advertising in all the media." By the same token, there are stations who have so many promotions going at one time that the listener literally becomes confused as to what is really happening. Obviously, the ideal situation is to strike a happy medium of not too much or too little. When and how and how much is the question each station has to answer for itself.

To properly understand station promotion as we know it today, it is important to understand its birth and growth. In the late 40s and early 50s, television became a power across the country. As television gained in popularity, radio's popularity declined. Many broadcasters and advertisers sat back and waited for radio to die. And dying it was. Radio had failed to meet the challenges of a new generation. For 30 years, it had been dominated by network programming including soap operas, quiz shows, music shows, all designed for people who had time on their hands and no other form of entertainment. Music on the local level was usually broadcast in 15 minute blocks and devoted to a 1930 or 1940 vocalist or band. Announcers with deep, resonant, and lifeless voices made station breaks, gave the time, and introduced records by Harry Horlick. The Ink Spots, Gordon Jenkins, and Guy Lombardo.

Glamourous television was upstaging radio, particularly those stations affiliated with the networks.

Then came the much needed shot in the arm: Top 40 radio. Todd Storz and Gordon McLendon were the early proponents of "exciting radio." Both were accused by fellow broadcasters of turning radio into an undignified electronic juke box. However, it wasn't long before these same broadcasters noted that the greater shares of audience and advertising dollars were being attracted to these "electronic juke boxes." And the big jump to the bandwagon began.

The innovators were suddenly competing with the imitators. And the innovations kept on coming, even to the point where it was almost amusing. When the innovator put a mobile news car on the streets, the imitator put two mobile news units on the streets. The innovator then added a mobile news boat, so the imitator added a boat and a mobile news airplane. The innovator would have a thousand dollar contest, so naturally the imitator would have a two thousand dollar contest. If the innovator gave away a trip to Miami, the imitator gave away a trip to Paris. And so it went. One gigantic game of "upmanship."

Competition in every market became keen and cut throat. Of course, it was inevitable that radio promotions would reach a limit and a saturation point, which it soon did. However, the excitement and the enthusiasm generated by radio promotions did not go unnoticed by the large consumer interested corporations. The large oil companies and giant grocery chains were quick to realize the importance of large scaled, large prized promotions and contests and they, too, jumped on the bandwagon.

In effect, the radio industry literally promoted itself out of the promotion business, at least as far as the giant giveaway was concerned. Thus radio promotion began to take on a new meaning and scope. Promotion directors and program directors suddenly realized that a good promotion did not have to cost an arm and a leg and, more importantly, they discovered that there was much more to promotion than just staging a contest.

PROMOTIONAL AIMS

Exactly what is a promotion and what should a promotion accomplish? To begin with, a promotion is not necessarily a contest. A promotion is any implemented idea or campaign which accomplishes any or all of the following: (a) enhances the station image, (b) increases the station's audience, (c) enables the station to increase its billing (there is no law which says a station can't sell a promotional idea to participating merchants), and (d) promotes the community or a community project.

In some cases promotion(s) is necessary to preserve and protect the station's image and position within the market. For example, in one large southern market a few years ago a contemporary station had enjoyed a long and successful leadership in the market. When a rival station changed format and began to challenge the leader, the challenged station found it necessary to almost triple its promotional budget to preserve its image and rating in the market.

What all the preceding amounts to is that a promotion just for promotion's sake is a useless and wasted effort. A promotion must have a definite purpose and goal, and the actual mechanics of the promotion must be geared to the accomplishment of that purpose and goal.

PLANNING A PROMOTION

There are three basic rules to consider to achieve a successful promotion: Timeliness, simplicity, and availability. The timeliness of a promotion is, of course, most important. You naturally do not stage a baseball oriented or related promotion at the end of the baseball season. For maximum penetration and effect, you stage a baseball related promotion at the beginning of the season when listener interest in that sport is high. Promotional tie-ins with holidays or special occasions are a must for any sharp station. It reflects the awareness of your station.

Simplicity is equally important. The more complicated a contest or promotion, the less likely it is to succeed. I've always used a rule of thumb, "Can it be explained **fully** in a 20-second promo?"

And third, availability. Will it be easy for the listener or respondent to participate in your promotion? Does the promotion have appeal to a majority? Or a minority?

However, your promotion may have timeliness, simplicity, and availability and still be a failure in every respect. The success or failure of any promotion is generally traceable, directly, to the amount of preparation that went into it. I've seen some of the greatest promotions bomb because the program director (in some cases—me) failed to properly prepare for the promotion. Proper preparation, with close attention to even the smallest detail, will greatly increase your chances for a successful promotion. Plan your promotion as if you were a general proceeding with a full-scale invasion.

Insure that every member of the radio station is thoroughly familiar with the mechanics of the entire promotion. Check your own experiences. How many times can you recall when a listener called a station or dropped by the office for details of something running on the air and the receptionist had to track down the program director to obtain an explanation. I've known many instances where listeners would come by a radio station to pick up a prize or make a recording in connection with a promotion and encounter total ignorance from every member of the staff. It is important that your preparation plans include "filling in" all personnel on what is happening.

Once the promotion is over, be sure you allow for follow-up action. If the promotion was a contest, let your audience know who the winners were. If the promotion was a community project or public service campaign, schedule promos to tell your audience what was accomplished. Be humble, but do not be afraid to subtly let the audience know how generous and great your station is. No matter how small a matter may seem upon the completion of a promotion, if it is in any way connected with the promotion, insure that the detail is handled.

Earlier we mentioned that a number of stations limit promotional efforts to their own facilities. This is the worst mistake a station can make. Many general managers feel that buying an ad or time on television or the newspaper is tantamount to admitting that radio cannot do the job. Exactly the opposite is true. Television and newspaper can be your most important tools in a promotional campaign. And don't forget those all important billboards. How in the world are you going to attract additional audience if you do not go outside your own medium to reach new people? If you restrict your promotional efforts to just your own station, you reach the same people over and over and over. Of course, you will receive the benefit of a small amount of word-of-mouth advertising, but the impact of this is insignificant. To insure the success of your promotion, it is advisable to utilize as much of the other media as practical and feasible.

BUDGET

I've been asked many times just how large a promotional budget a station should maintain from month to month or year to year. This is a very difficult question to answer. There are too many factors to be taken into consideration, and situations differ from market to market. Your position of strength in the market, the economic condition of your station, the size of your market, the number of competing signals within your primary coverage area—these are all factors that have to be considered before establishing any promotional budget. And many times you are really unable to have a firm figure given to your department. It depends on the individual program director's ability to sell the general manager on what the station should do from month to month. Many program directors prefer to have an amount available each and every month. Some, including myself, prefer to have a flexible system which can be increased or decreased as the situation demands. The important thing is to have access to some promotional money. To survive in a competitive market, you have to promote.

8   The Disc Jockey

Al Jarvis and Martin Block were the first disc jockeys of any importance. And since those days of the early 30s, the disc jockey has been maligned, praised, cursed, pleaded with, investigated, glorified, underpaid, overpaid, insulted, underated, overrated, neglected, tolerated, appreciated, spoiled, hated, idolized, taken advantage of, and worshipped. Salesmen tolerate him, general managers search for him, program directors plead with him, secretaries fall in love with him, listeners idolize him, clients need him, and engineers deplore him. He's been called Star, VIP, Big Man, Personality, Mr. Big, Mr. Music, Mr. Phoney, Robot, Professional, Amateur, Bush, Big League, and yet no matter what the nomenclature—he is, has been, and always will be "what it's all about." He is radio. The public doesn't know anything about formats, formulas, music lists, salesmen, managers, program directors, engineers, traffic girls, or secretaries. Radio is the **disc jockey.**

Most dictionaries define disc jockey as a commentator or host of a music show. I prefer to think of a disc jockey as a communicator. Because that is, in essence, what he is paid to do—to communicate. And the definition of communicate? The Reader's Digest Great Encyclopedic Dictionary says, "Communicate is to cause another or others to partake of or share in." How, then do you develop this art or science of communication?

The greatest sin committed by the majority of disc jockeys is that they fail to work at being a disc jockey. This failure to work automatically puts a DJ in the position of betraying a trust. A trust to themselves, to their station, and more importantly, to their listeners. A disc jockey's failure to work is a flagrant, inexcusable disregard of responsiblilty.

Immediately, every disc jockey reading this will say to himself, "I'm glad this doesn't apply to me." Well, perhaps it does apply to you. Maybe you are not quite as proficient as you think you are. Let's discover how well you know and practice your craft and see if you are a disc jockey or just an announcer. The following Disc Jockey Proficiency and Evaluation Test should help you determine your true worth as a DJ. But remember, be honest and objective. The only one who will know the answer is you and the only person hurt by a dishonest answer is yourself. There are 35 questions. Each question has three possible answers A, B, C. Mark your selection in the space provided in the right-hand margin. Answer as quickly as you can and be as honest as you can.

DISC JOCKEY PROFICIENCY AND EVALUATION TEST

1. As a DJ, do you consider yourself knowledgeable in the area of FCC Rules and Regulations?
    (a) Know thoroughly
    (b) Have a working knowledge
    (c) Familiar with   _____
2. How well do you adhere to FCC Rules and Regulations?
    (a) Always (b) Occasionally (c) Often lax   _____
3. How well do you adhere to company rules and regulations?
    (a) Always (b) Occasionally lax (c) Often lax   _____
4. How well do you carry out assigned duties?
    (a) Promptly
    (b) As soon as time permits
    (c) Have to be reminded   _____
5. How well do you follow the station format?
    (a) Never deviate
    (b) Occasionally deviate
    (c) Have to be reminded   _____
6. Do you play only your favorite records?
    (a) Never (b) Occasionally (c) Yes   _____
7. Are you always "up" for your program?
    (a) Always
    (b) Occasionally down
    (c) Only with stimulants   _____

8. How much time do you spend in selecting music for your program?
  (a) More than 30 minutes
  (b) Less than 30 minutes
  (c) None _____

9. How knowledgeable are you about music and records?
  (a) Very (b) Some (c) None _____

10. Do you show this knowledge of music on the air?
  (a) Whenever possible (b) Occasionally (c) Never _____

11. As a DJ, do you restrict your on-the-air comments to only time, temp, weather, record intros, and name credit?
  (a) Never (b) Occasionally (c) Always _____

12. Do you use jokes or one-liners on the air?
  (a) Many (b) Occasionally (c) Never _____

13. Do you use informative bits on the air?
  (a) Often (b) Occasionally (c) Never _____

14. How much actual time do you spend in preparing your show?
  (a) More than 1 hour
  (b) More than 30 minutes
  (c) Less than 30 minutes _____

15. Do you always know what you're going to say before you open the mike or do you just wing it?
  (a) Always know (b) Vaguely (c) Wing it _____

16. Do you read all the trade magazines and publications regularly?
  (a) Always (b) Occasionally (c) Never _____

17. Are you involved in the community?
  (a) Very much (b) Some (c) No _____

18. How many personal appearances did you make last month?
  (a) More than 5 (b) More than 1 (c) None _____

19. How many people do you talk to on the telephone, during your program?
  (a) More than 25 (b) Less than 25 (c) None _____

20. Have you ever come to work with a hangover?
  (a) Never (b) Once (c) Occasionally _____

21. Do people recognize you as being a DJ when you are introduced?

    (a) Always (b) Most of the time (c) Occasionally ———

22. Do advertisers request your talent and voice on commercials?

    (a) Regularly (b) Occasionally (c) No ———

23. How much market research have you done on your own the last 30 days?

    (a) A great deal (b) Some (c) None ———

24. How well do you like your present job?

    (a) Very much (b) So-so (c) Am looking ———

25. How many civic clubs or organizations do you belong to?

    (a) More than 1 (b) One (c) None ———

26. How many programming suggestions did you submit to the PD in connection with your program last month?

    (a) More then 1 (b) One (c) None ———

27. How many technical mistakes do you average per show?

    (a) None (b) One (c) More than 1 ———

28. How many magazines do you read each week?

    (a) More than one (b) One (c) None ———

29. Do you thoroughly read the newspaper every day?

    (a) Regularly

    (b) Occasionally

    (c) At least twice a week ———

30. Do you pre-read copy and news before broadcast?

    (a) Always

    (b) Occasionally

    (c) If there is time ———

31. How often do you tape your show in order to critique your program?

    (a) Every week

    (b) At least every two weeks

    (c) Once a month ———

32. Do you try to pattern your style after a particular DJ?

    (a) No (b) A little (c) Yes ———

33. Do you steal ad libs from other DJs?

    (a) No (b) Occasionally (c) Yes ———

34. Do you ever conduct any music or record research in order to determine who is buying what?

(a) Regularly (b) Occasionally (c) No ⎯⎯⎯

35. Are you the best DJ at your station?

(a) Yes (b) No (c) Second best ⎯⎯⎯

Now, add up your answers. How many A⎯? B⎯? C⎯? If you had more than one B and more than one C, your proficiency as a disc jockey would have to be considered sub-par. No matter how long you've been in the business or how much money you are presently making or what your ratings are, if you had more than one B and more than one C you have not taken your chosen craft seriously. You are coasting.

So much for the test. Let's try, now, to improve your proficiency rating. The remainder of this chapter is designed to do just that: Raise your proficiency and stimulate you into becoming a real professional.

DISC JOCKEY TYPES OR CLASSIFICATIONS

What type DJ are you? Whenever I've asked this question I've generally received the same answer, "I'm not a DJ. I'm a personality." All right, what type of personality are you? I've yet to receive an acceptable answer. The dictionary defines personality as "one who possesses outstanding or distinctive qualities." I would define personality as "one who possesses that X factor which the audience or listener can immediately identify with or respond to." I can't tell you what that X factor is. It's very much like electricity. You know it's there but you can't really describe it.

Personality can't be really defined, but the term disc jockey can. In my opinion there are eight classifications or types of DJs. I'm sure that number could be expanded to include as many as four, five, or even six additional types. However, these eight categories or types cover the majority of announcers in the business today. Let's find out what type you are or want to be.

1. **The time and temperature jock:** Often called the robot or the button pusher. Most abundant of all DJ species and in most cases because of management. Managers, particularly in small and medium markets, are afraid of hiring or

developing a personality type jock. They have found that once a DJ begins to exhibit any sort of talent for saying anything other than time and temperature, it's only a matter of time before a larger station lures him away. However, there is an additional point to consider. When a DJ first starts out, there is a natural tendency to "keep one foot in the mouth." Oftentimes, these ill-timed quips and ad libs create waves and the small market manager tries to keep the waves down to a minimum by instituting a "time and temperature policy" only.

I do want to point out, though, that time and temperature jocks are not restricted to just small or medium markets. They are to be found in abundance in the largest of markets. Formats dictate what a DJ can or cannot say and many formats are so restrictive that it is impossible to be anything other than a time and temperature jock.

Many young DJs have asked me how they can develop a style or talent if the format is so restrictive as to prevent them from doing anything other than time and temp. My advice is to take very small steps at a time. For the sake of explanation, let's say that a young DJ wants to tell jokes on the air, but the manager says no. The thing to do is find an exceptionally timely and funny one-liner and rehearse the ad lib until you have the delivery perfected. Then make an audition tape illustrating how the one-liner would sound on the air. Ask the manager to listen to your tape and then ask if you can tell that joke on your next show. If he says yes, you've won the first round. The next day try two one-liners on your tape and then three, and four, etc. The important thing is to win his trust. Once you have done this, you'll find that more and more liberties are available to you.

However, suppose the manager says no to your audition tape. Then you have your work cut out for you. You are going to have to sell the manager. And the easiest way to sell him is through hard work. Don't try a verbal sales pitch. Young DJs do not have the experience to match wits with a good salesman. Through hard work you can get that manager so obligated to you that he'll be ashamed to say no to a request to tell "just this one joke." And as you keep working diligently (above and beyond the call of duty), keep asking for leeway or permission to tell more jokes, just a few at a time. You'll soon win his confidence and trust concerning your ability on the air, not to mention the raise you'll get because of all that work.

One thing I want to make clear is that it's wrong to assume that a time and temp jock is not a personality. He still possesses that quality which an individual can identify with or respond to. He may be a personality because of the music he plays or the station he's working for, or because of both. Some of the biggest personalities in our business are time and temp jocks. Generally, though, they are big because of what they do when they are not on the air. Later in this chapter I discuss what to do off the air to become a personality in a restrictive format.

2. **The live wire:** He is exactly what the name implies. He may tell jokes, editorialize, or be a musicologist, but basically he is the enthusiastic go-getter. Enthusiasm is contagious and the live wire is able to transmit his enthusiasm to his listener and, perhaps more importantly, to the staff. Every station needs at least one live wire if only to keep everyone's adrenalin flowing.

3. **The voice:** This type DJ is becoming less and less common. Having that big, beautiful, resonant voice doesn't necessarily qualify anyone for today's radio scene. In fact, many program directors consider a beautiful, articulate voice a handicap. Who can identify with perfection? If you are depending on your voice alone to carry you up the ladder, I would suggest that you seriously consider moving into the television field. The voice is no longer a necessity for radio.

4. **The comedian:** This type is quite distinctive. He's the guy with a joke or two for every subject and situation. To be a comedian requires a great deal of work and preparation. I know of some DJs who merely subscribe to the various joke services and the only work or preparation they perform is opening the envelope containing the jokes. There is much more to being a comedian on the air than just reading jokes from a comedy service. There are certain rules to observe in order to qualify as a professional radio comedian.

Rule one. Decide which type comedy you can perform best. Are you a wit, a humorist, story teller, clown, or satirist. These are the basic types and very few DJs can be adept in all categories. So, determine which type or types of comedy you can most effectively put across and concentrate in these areas.

Rule two. Determine what is funny and what is funny for you; the two do not necessarily go together. I've always made it an ironclad rule of telling jokes on the air that I think are funny. I'm sure that, over the years, I could have told an additional ten thousand jokes, but those ten thousand were not funny to me; therefore, I could not effectively tell them. Do not use a joke just because it is classified as a joke. Use only those jokes which are funny to you.

Rule three. Whenever possible, localize your joke or material. Tell the joke in such a way as to enable the listener to relate with it. For example, take this average one-liner and watch what happens: "About the time a man stops drinking and swearing, Congress comes up with another big budget." Now, let's take the same line and localize it in such a manner that your listener can immediately relate with it. "About the time a man stops drinking and swearing, our city fathers come up with another budget or bond issue." The joke doesn't become any funnier; it only becomes more easy for the listener to relate with. Whenever possible, use local names, groups, staff members, and even advertisers. Most people have a sense of humor and as long as you are not derogatory, you'll encounter no problems.

In using advertisers, however, be careful. One safe way is to not use them in a joke but credit them with having told you a joke. This technique can be very effective in establishing your talent with clients. Localization gives your material new dimensions and a joke or one-liner becomes funnier when you use a name or place that fits the situation. Instead of just saying, "a drunk was expelled from Alcoholics Anonymous because he wasn't anonymous enough to suit them," use the name of a DJ on your staff—or your boss. With the proper use of material which has been localized, you can even create personalities on your program. In one market where I worked, the station had a particularly well-endowed, good-looking secretary. I gave her the name of Sam and every joke I could write or find concerning fat or ugly or untalented girls, I used in connection with Sam. She never went on the air, but everyone in town soon knew her name. She became an additional "personality" on the staff. Listeners actually called her everyday to suggest ways to "get back at me." Her presence gave my program a new dimension, the station a new personality, and the listener someone else to relate with. Localize your material.

Rule four Practice. Rehearse your material. Never try to tell a joke unless you've rehearsed and rehearsed it. Confidence assures you of your ability and practice gives you confidence.

Rule five. Develop your timing. Before you tell a story, figure out where to pause or how to strike home with the punch line. Professional comedians have a trick laugh or look just before they deliver the punch line. The DJ must use the slight pause and when the punch line is delivered, he can't wait for the laugh. He's got to be on top of the punch line with a jingle or a record. Perfect your timing. And once the punch line is delivered don't elaborate. Play a record.

Rule six. Establish a gag file. Every time you discover a joke worth using on the air, type it on a 3 x 5 card and file the card away, because in six months you can rewrite the joke and use it again. For easy reference, I would suggest that you categorize your material.

If you want to be a professional radio comedian, be prepared for long hours of research and preparation. And also be prepared for big pay checks because the professional radio comedians can demand them.

5. **The social critic:** In many cases, is also a satirist. His ad lib comments range from priests getting married, to air pollution, to the city council. He relies, primarily, on the daily newspaper for his material and no person or institution is safe from his attacks. It is not uncommon to hear him use humor in the form of one-liners to drive a point home. It has been my experience that no one person on a staff can create as much comment, good and bad, as the social critic. No listener is ever neutral over him. They either hate him or love him. He will attract both admirers and critics with his controversial comments and he oftentimes is guilty of skating on very thin ice. Social critics have been known to sway elections, improve traffic conditions, build roads, expose corruption, obtain pardons for criminals, influence politicians, build hospitals—and lose sponsors. They've also been known to be fired at the drop of a hat—or letter from an influential client. Unfortunately, very few station managers have the intestinal fortitude necessary to live with a social critic. It indeed takes guts to be this type of disc jockey and if this is your "thing," ratings and fat pay checks will come your way—if you can master the technique of knowing just how far you can or cannot go.

6. **The musicologist** is the guy who is really into the music. The "good" musicologist spends a great deal of time in research and he is not content to know where a song was recorded and who the musicians are. He wants to know who wrote the song, why the song was written, and why the singer is recording the song. In other words, he wants information that will not only be entertaining but provocative.

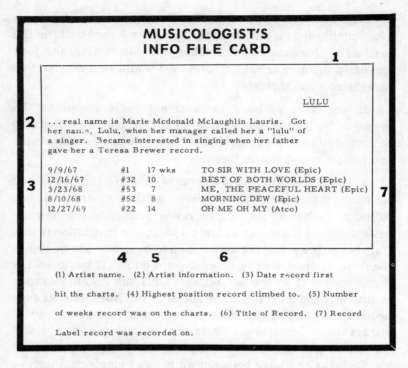

MUSICOLOGIST'S INFO FILE CARD

1

LULU

2 ...real name is Marie Mcdonald Mclaughlin Lauris. Got her name, Lulu, when her manager called her a "lulu" of a singer. Became interested in singing when her father gave her a Teresa Brewer record.

3

9/9/67	#1	17 wks	TO SIR WITH LOVE (Epic)
12/16/67	#32	10	BEST OF BOTH WORLDS (Epic)
3/23/68	#53	7	ME, THE PEACEFUL HEART (Epic)
8/10/68	#52	8	MORNING DEW (Epic)
12/27/69	#22	14	OH ME OH MY (Atco)

7

4   **5**   **6**

(1) Artist name. (2) Artist information. (3) Date record first hit the charts. (4) Highest position record climbed to. (5) Number of weeks record was on the charts. (6) Title of Record. (7) Record Label record was recorded on.

He collects newspaper clippings, magazine articles, trade reports, comments from record promotion men, and sometimes he even collects information direct from the artist. He searches and digs for the unusual little tidbit that will enable him to introduce a record with more than just the artist's name and song title. Musicologists have probably been responsible for breaking in more new or unknown records and artists than any other type disc jockey. Their knowledge of the artist, record, and lyrics enables the listener to really get into a record and understand it.

Card files are an essential tool for the musicologist. Information is easily transferred to a card, thereby making the information readily available for reference and use.

The only drawback to being a musicologist, other than the work involved, is that oftentimes he has a tendency to give too much information which, of course, creates a tune-out factor, not to mention the chewing out from the program director for talking too much. Musicologists are also inclined to get carried away, since it's not unusual for them to feel as if they must say something about **every** artist and record they program. Avoid this pitfall. Keep your comments short, brief, to the point, and **don't overdo it.**

7. **The guy next door** is just that. He is a warm, believable, sincere, family man. Occasionally, he's funny, but he's never controversial and more often he's the guy who is fighting the same problems as the listener. He has troubles with parking tickets, garbage collectors, check-out clerks, TV, his wife, his kids, the boss and city hall. He's having trouble with his car, his house needs painting, he can't potty-train his son, and his wife sent his favorite jacket to the Goodwill Industries. Listeners can really relate with him and his ratings and demographics prove it. However, he sometimes has a tendency to talk too much. Unlike most DJs, it is rather hard for him to rehearse his ad libs. He has notes on what he plans to talk about, but to keep the sound believable, he has to wing it and, as we said, sometimes talks himself into a corner and into trouble with the program director. If you follow this path, be careful you don't talk too much.

8. **The total entertainer** is the guy who can do it all. He's all types roled into one heavy professional radio man. He spends so much time preparing "bits" for his program that he hardly has time for anything else. The total entertainer is probably the most dedicated of all disc jockeys. And his take home pay every month reflects this dedication. To me, he epitomizes the DJ. They do not just happen overnight. Dues have been paid for years and finally the long, extra hours pay off with a shot at the "big gig." If you have a goal, shoot for the total entertainer.

Eight types or classifications of disc jockeys. Which do you fit into? Well, regardless of your classification, there are other factors to weigh before you may consider yourself a pro. And that's what we're going to examine now, the factors which determine the success of every disc jockey.

SHOW PREPARATION

How much time do you devote each day to the preparation of your program? Three hours? An hour? Thirty minutes?

How about ten minutes? I firmly believe that it is impossible to do a 3-hour program without a minimum of two hours preparation. And many top flight DJs and program directors suggest a minimum of two hours—FOR **EVERY HOUR YOU ARE ON THE AIR.** I would be willing to wager that more than 80 percent of the nation's disc jockeys go on the air without any preparation whatsoever. They simply prance into the control room a minute before air time, exchange insults with the man on duty, then plop down into that easy chair for three hours of "faking it." And when you go on the air without preparation, that is what you are doing—faking it! And when you fake it, you are cheating your audience, your station, and yourself.

I believe it was Woodrow Wilson who once said, "If I have to speak an hour, I can do it right now. However, if my speech is to be only ten minutes, I will need several days to prepare." Therein lies the reason for preparation. Under the rigid formats of today when you have only a few seconds between records for conversation, it is even more important that you prepare and rehearse your ad libs. I've had young jocks tell me they didn't need to prepare their programs because they were better "off the cuff" or "off the top of the head." This may be true in about two cases in a hundred. The average jock today, if he is going to effectively communicate with his audience, needs preparation for his program. Look at it this way. In one 3-hour stint, in a normal format with a normal commercial load, a disc jockey will have approximately twelve opportunities to express himself. Multiply this by three hours and you have 36 occasions to wing a comment off the top of your head. If you can rise to the occasion 36 times a day, five days a week, you're wasting your talents as a disc jockey. You ought to be writing speeches for the president or telling Bob Hope how to do his thing.

Every trade magazine you read these days bemoans the lack of personalities in radio. I disagree with the idea that there is a lack of personalities. I believe there is just a lack of people willing to dedicate themselves to their chosen craft. Have you ever heard Charley Tuna, Don Rose, George Michaels, Larry Lujack, Gary Owens, Jay Lawrence, Jim

LaBarbara, Harvey Hudson, Pat Patterson, Ty Boyd, Paul Henning, Don Imus, just to name a few of the nation's outstanding personalities? Do you think that they go on the air and "wing it?" If they did, they would sound just like thousands of other disc jockeys across the country—a pleasant voice giving time and temperature. As it is, they put work into their programs and you can detect the difference. Their programs are professional, entertaining, informative, and in keeping with today's world. Their programs are alive.

How do you prepare a show? For some reason this is probably the most guarded secret (other than formats) in the industry. No one ever volunteered to teach me or even give a pointer or two. I learned (stole) a little from Harvey Hudson (WLEE–Richmond) and then developed my own system. I think, perhaps, that ego has a little to do with the secrecy. Most personalities, including myself, are hesitant to admit that those clever ad libs aren't as spontaneous as they sound. At any rate, I'm going to give you a typical "prep sheet" as prepared and used by me. The illustration may serve as a guide to help you develop your own system and prep sheet. You will notice that various entries on the prep sheet have been numbered so we can refer to them here.

1. The date and day. This eliminates any possibility of forgetting the date or day and sounding stupid. It also serves as a reminder. Every jock always remembers to give the day, but for some reason the date is seldom given. I always gave it, as a service to people who might be writing checks that day. (Last time you wrote a check did you have to stop and think about what date it was?)

2. Just a reminder that the date is Columbus Day.

3. Time or hour the sheet was to be used. I prepared one sheet per hour.

4. This column is for the commercials scheduled for the hour. I always had the traffic girl make an extra copy of my portion of the log. There are three entries in the column; client name, cart number, and length of the commercial. You will notice that the commercials are pre-grouped for clustering (eight clusters per hour) to eliminate having to figure out the

1 Date _Oct. 12_ , _Friday_ _Columbus Day_ TIME _7AM-8AM_

6 RECORDS: _1-23- X1 - 7 - G - 5 - 31 - 28 - 40 - 2 - G 14-G_

7 TODAY IS RODERIGO DE TRIANA DAY. AND
ALL THE TIME YOU THOUGHT IT WAS
COLUMBUS DAY. BUT IT WAS REALLY
RODERIGO, A SAILOR ABOARD THE PINTA,
WHO SIGHTED WATLING ISLAND IN THE
WEST INDIES, WHICH CC CLAIMED IN THE
NAME OF FERDINAND AND ISABELLA.

CC DISCOVERED NOT ONLY AMERICA,
BUT THE CACAO BEAN. SPAIN KEPT
THE ART OF MAKING CHOCOLATE A
SECRET FROM THE REST OF EUROPE
FOR ALMOST 100 YEARS. IT SOLD FOR
THREE DOLLARS A POUND, SO ONLY
THE RICH COULD DRINK IT.

8 What a politician Columbus would have
been in this day and age. When he started
out he didn't know where he was going.
When he got there he didn't know where
he was... and when he got back he didn't
know where he'd been... and he did all
this on the government's money.

Tried that new cocktail....the Christopher
Columbus Cocktail. Two and you discover
a new world.

9 Robert E. Lee died (1870).. National
Industrial week begins (12-18)... Jewish
Hold Day, Simchat Torah or rejoicing
of the law...Nat'l School Lunchweek
continues...National pharmacy Week.....

10 I've got to move. The walls in my
apartment are so thin that when my
wife peels onions, the guy next door cries.

Ready for a mystery? After you give
up smoking, what happens to the money
you used to spend on cigarettes.

11 Sam is wearing a sweater today. That's
a waste. About the only thing a sweater
does for her is to make her itch.....

13 _J.P. @ 2 PM_

12 NAMES:

And Richards - Telephone Co.
Mayor Stevens - Birthday ⑤③ .
Mark Taylor - Cook @ Holiday Inn

4
Ford	- 101	- 60
Ames	75	- 60
Maola	14	- 20
Center	78	- 20
Johnson	65	- 60 _3:10_
Marks	201	- 30
Amber	10	- 60 _3:00_
Clark	74	- 60 _4:00_
Wilson	18	- 20
Mack	16	- 20
Johnson	64	- 20

ALLen's 22-60 **5**

Dodge	200	- 60
Coke	151	- 30
Marks	201	- 30
Blue fl	84	- 60 _3 ½ mins_
Pizza hut	60	- 30
Rogers	82	- 30
Arnolds	181	- 60
Bakers	190	- 60
Helmer	3	- 30
Jackson	90	- 30 _3:40_
Maola	14	- 20
Johnson	64	- 20

U.S. Bombers
Hit Laos **15**
Kennedy says No

Lion's Club Broom
Sale begin tom - **14**

cluster sequence during the show. I've also indicated the length in minutes of each cluster.

5. This spot had to be added after I had received the copy of the master log. You always need to double check the log for possible write-ins, which will, of course, have to be added to the prep sheet.

6. Denotes the records selected for play during that hour. By preselecting the records, it is not necessary to waste any time during the program trying to decide what to play. They are listed in the sequence called for by the format.

7. I call these "pseudo intellectual" drop-ins, or just plain informational tidbits. It was Columbus Day so the information was selected to fit the occasion. It came from my files which contains information for every special day and week of the year. The information is typed in all caps to serve as a reminder that the bit is to be used over a record intro. You will note the arrow to record XI. I know from this entry that record X1 has a 17-second musical intro which will allow me enough time to read the bit before the vocal starts.

8. Naturally, jokes and one liners pertaining to Columbus Day.

9. From my files. A complete day-by-day account of what happened in history on each date and what is happening on that particular day.

10. Regular one-liners to work into the program. Since all my material was on 3 x 5 cards, I always had 10 to 20 additional one-liners handy in case I needed more material during the program.

11. Remember Sam under the comedian disc jockey category?

12. Names of people in the community. I always dropped at least ten names a day representing people from all walks of life. People I knew, heard about, or read about. If they were listening, it was quite a surprise to hear their name on the radio. And if they were not listening, invariably someone would tell them that they heard their name on the Raleigh show.

13. My "DJ of the day." Each day, rather than the normal DJ cross plugs, I would use a DJ in several one-liners to showcase the cross plug.

14. A last-minute telephone call from a civic club to plug a fund-raising event.

15. Two quickie news headlines, in case I wanted to plug the upcoming newscast.

As I stated earlier, this is the system I used for over ten years as a morning man. I haven't the slightest idea what system others might use so I have no way of knowing whether my system is a good one or not. I do know that it worked for me. Devise your own system. The important thing is **show preparation**. Without it, you're just another voice on the radio.

THE SHOW MUST GO ON

Professionalism dictates that no matter what your mood, no matter what troubles you may have, no matter what, **a pro is up for his show.** When that mike is opened, all thoughts of personal problems, hangovers, headaches, chewing outs, or what have you are forgotten. Unfortunately, too many of today's disc jockeys lack this sense of professionalism. Far too often, the disc jockey's mood determines the mood and tempo of his program. Your listeners have their own problems and they are not particularly interested in yours. They dial in on the station for one reason—to escape or to be entertained.

Pride should dictate your moods, really. You must have enough pride to put forth your very best effort every day. I once worked with a jock who was utterly fantastic. He was funny, he was quick-witted, enthusiastic; in fact, he was everything you could possibly want in a DJ—one day a week. The other four days he sounded as if he had lost his best friend. He had no pride in his performance during that period and absolutely no respect from the rest of the staff. Such a talent, but he had no sense of professionalism. Earlier we mentioned that enthusiasm is contagious. Well, remember this: so are the blues.

KNOW YOUR AUDIENCE

Many disc jockeys today haven't the slightest idea who they are reaching. To them, the audience consists of just people. To be truly effective as a DJ, it is imperative to think of the audience as "individuals." How can you converse or communicate with someone if you do not have any idea of who they are, what they think, their likes and dislikes, age, sex, and background? And before you can begin to learn about your audience, you first have to learn about the market.

The very first thing anyone should do upon arriving in a new market is to go to the public library and spend some time reading up on the history of the market. Once you have absorbed some historical background, move into the economical, geographical, and political areas of the community. Also, you should visit the Chamber of Commerce and obtain any literature available on the community. I'm not suggesting you take a cram course in order to be an authority; rather, I am suggesting you obtain, as quickly as possible, a feel for the market. Once you have completed this phase of market research, begin to learn of the people. Find out who lives in the market and why. Talk to people everywhere you go, and don't be bashful. Introduce yourself. Spread your name over the entire community.

I have a checklist of people I try to visit within the first four weeks of my arrival in a new market. Here is the list and the reason I try to talk with them.

1. **Mayor.** He can give you a capsule report on the current problems and goals of the community.

2. **City Council Member(s).** I try to talk to at least two. Not only can they verify the mayor's report, they can give you an insight into their own special goals and pet projects for the city.

3. **Police Chief.** He can give you a capsule report on the police department and its problems.

4. **Democratic and Republican Party Chairmen.** You'll learn which party is the power in the city and much about the voters.

5. **Human Relations Director.** Discuss with him the racial problems (if any) and obtain the names of several minority community leaders to meet.

6. **School Board Member(s).** Learn about the school enrollment, schools, teachers, school problems, etc.

7. **Church Council President or Pastor.** He can tell you about the religious community in the city.

8. **Boys Club, Boy Scouts, YMCA, Parks & Recreation Director, etc.** Each is a valuable source of information concerning youth activities.

9. **Dean of Admissions** (if there is a University). Find out where the students come from, college activities, etc. You can also get your name on the mailing list so you'll receive future announcements and news releases.

10. **Chamber of Commerce.** Get all available literature on the market and talk with the chamber secretary. Also ask for a report on industry, which will reveal where people work and what time they go to and from work. Also obtain a list of scheduled events and a list of all civic clubs and their presidents.

After meeting and talking with the above people, you will probably know as much about the market as the average resident. But the job is not finished. You still have to **meet** the people. The quickest way is by use of the telephone. I've never worked at a station where I did not have a direct line into the control room (sometimes it took quite a bit of salesmanship on my part to convince the manager that a phone was important). A telephone enables you to have direct contact with your audience. It can be the most valuable tool you'll have in establishing rapport with your listeners. And it will not interfere with your show, if you have prepared your show!

In any 3-hour program I can talk to a minimum of 30 people. Multiply 30 people a day times five days and you have talked to 150 listeners by the end of the week. Or 7,500 "one-on-one" contacts in a year. Of course, many are repeat contacts, but that is still a lot of "cumes." The phone enables you to win friends and influence listening. However, it is not a request line. I have never taken a request. I would "hype" the phone with quickie quizzes, calls for birthdays and anniversaries, and one of the quickest ways to motivate the listener into calling you is to make a deliberate mistake on the air. The deluge of listeners calling to correct the mistake will begin as soon as the mike is closed. And you'll even sound more human by making the mistake. Another phone ploy is to play dumb as if you cannot remember what year some gold record was popular. Again, that phone will ring as someone calls to give you the information.

However, the phone is not intended to improve your after-hours social life. Keep your conversation pleasant, appreciative, congenial, and short. Chat briefly with your listeners. Find out about them. Develop a concept of your audience and then translate that knowledge into your air delivery to an individual. Radio is still—and always will be—**one on one**. So, know your market.

PERSONAL CONTACT WITH YOUR AUDIENCE

No matter what type DJ you are, it is still important to be personally involved in the community. This means that it is important that you get out and meet the people and let them meet you. Sometimes it is necessary for you to take the initiative on your own if your station lacks agressive management.

Throughout this book I've purposely avoided as much as possible mentioning names of people I've come in contact with or worked with. However, I have to make an exception again for Harvey Hudson (WLEE-Richmond). For years, Harvey made it a practice to visit hospital patients every Sunday. Following church and dinner, Harvey would head for the hospital. Once there he visited as many rooms as possible. He just walked into a room, introduced himself, inquired of the patient's health, wished him or her a speedy recovery, and proceeded to another room. This was just one of the reasons Harv was able to remain the number one disc jockey for over a quarter of a century, and at a salary you wouldn't believe. Harvey has spent his career meeting listeners and he taught me a very valuable lesson. Once an individual meets you in person, you cease to be just a voice on the radio. You become a real person. You become something a little special. Meet enough people and become a special individual to enough people in a market and no one will be able to touch you in the ratings.

There are many ways you can get out and establish personal contact. If there is a college in your market, volunteer your services to emcee any events that may be scheduled. You might drop a note to all civic clubs and advise them that you are available as an emcee and guest speaker. Civic clubs are always looking for speakers and it will give you an opportunity to develop close, personal contact with the members. I would suggest, as your speech theme, a short talk on how to obtain free advertising and publicity from radio stations for the club's various projects. Contact the local high schools and volunteer to visit the school's speech classes to give a talk on radio as a career. Volunteer to do remote broadcasts. You'll meet hundreds of people and be able to "sell" yourself to the man who sponsored the remote broadcast (for future talent checks when he requests your services on commercials and other remotes). Watch the paper for special "free" classes conducted by the city. I once received a special award and mileage galore when I enrolled in a city-sponsored knitting class (I was the only male student).

I could go on and on, and so can you. Always be on the alert for any opportunity to get yourself before the public. And be sure to drop a little thank you note to the organization after your appearance.

Should you charge for these appearances? That is a question each DJ has to answer himself. I never charged anyone except profit-making organizations. If a local promoter brings in a group and wants an emcee, he should be charged. However, the effort you make to appear at all other functions will be amply rewarded by raises you receive as your ratings climb. Establish personal contact with your audience. If they meet you, they'll listen to you. It's as simple as that.

DIRECTION AND CORRECTION EQUALS PERFECTION

How often do you tape your program in order to have it critiqued, either by you or the program director? You should

d analyze what you are doing at least once a week.
r pacing, your direction, and particularly your ad
d you have rephrased an ad lib in another way in
cut out excess words and gotten to the point
Are you walking on records? How's the sound level
st between voice and music? There are a thousand
you can improve on every week, but you'll never know
they are until you make a tape of your show.

Unfortunately, most disc jockeys (including this writer),
have the inability to listen with as critical an ear as a disinterested party. So it is advisable to have someone sit in on the critique session with you. And, I repeat, you should have your program critiqued at least **once a week**. It is so very easy to get into a rut or develop little cliches or crutches that are not immediately evident. I would also suggest that you dispense with any mental masturbation. Forget how great you sound, how smooth the program is, or how witty you are. Pick the program to pieces. And don't be sensitive when your program is criticized. I've known so many young jocks who were totally unable to take criticism.

To help you in your weekly program critiques, I have prepared the following check list. I would suggest you keep a copy in your brief case for reference.

CRITIQUE CHECK LIST

1. Too much time and temperature? Is it becoming a crutch?
2. Too much repetition of weather? A crutch?
3. Too much mention of day and date?
4. Any repetition of pet phrases?
5. Are you talking over every record intro?
6. Are you clipping records short by beginning to talk too soon?
7. Are your record intros always the same?
8. Are you talking too fast?
9. Are you talking too slow?
10. Are you talking too much? Or too little?
11. Are you talking in a monotone?

12. Are you talking "to" or "at" your audience?

13. Is your music balanced?

14. Is there any shuffling of papers, carts, etc., on mike?

15. Are you too tight with your commercial clusters?

16. Is there any dead air?

17. Are you laughing too much at your own jokes?

18. Is your diction and pronunciation clear?

19. Are you talking off mike at any time?

20. Are the records clean or scratchy?

21. Are the cart machines and tape machines clean?

22. Is separation of competitive sponsors satisfactory?

23. How is the sound level relationship from voice to music to commercial?

24. How is the level between voice and music when talking over record intros?

25. How is the level between voice and music when talking over record closes?

26. Is the music right for your target audience?

27. Is there any evidence of not being prepared?

28. Are you cross plugging DJs and programs?

29. Are you delivering your punch lines effectively?

30. Did you back time the last record before the news?

31. Could you have rephrased your ad libs in order to be more brief?

32. Does your program flow? Or is it jerky?

33. Do you use "uh" when ad libbing?

34. Are you using the word "about" (about 60 degrees or about 10:30)?

35. Are you sounding positive or negative?

36. Are commercial clusters too long?

37. Are jingles clear, showcased, and properly rotated?

38. Are you drowning jingles with voice or record?

39. Do you sound happy? Enthusiastic?

40. Are you improving?

DJ DOs AND DON'Ts

By following the suggestions listed below, a DJ can avoid a lot of trouble. Chances are the station will have a list already prepared. However, if they do not, the following will help you.

1. Don't ever have alcoholic beverages on the station premises.

2. Don't make any long distance calls and charge them to the station telephone under any circumstances.

3. Don't allow visitors in the control room or in the station while you are on duty.

4. Don't make any purchases without authorization from the program director or general manager.

5. Don't bring personal records or equipment to the station.

6. Do be neatly groomed at all times. Remember you are a representative of the radio station.

7. Do manage your personal affairs in such a manner as to be above reproach in the community.

8. Do fill out your transmitter and program logs properly and completely.

9. Do be familiar with the procedures for taking meter readings.

10. Do be familiar with the EBS and EAN system.

11. Do know how to call and who to call to report remote line troubles, news line troubles or network troubles.

12. Do note all discrepancies observed during your shift.

13. Do follow the prescribed format. Do not deviate in any manner unless authorization has been given by the program director.

14. Do avoid redundancy on the air. Ex.: Repeating pet phrases or introing the intros.

15. Do avoid superimposing your voice over your recorded voice situations.

16. Do be familiar with the pronunciation of names and words. Ask.

17. Do clear the newswire at least every 30 munutes while you are on duty.

18. Do be informative. Use items that will be of interest to your listeners.

19. Don't telegraph news, sports, weather, features, etc. Avoid phrases such as, "And now to carry us up to the news, here's so and so to sing, etc...."

20. Do be prepared before your record ends. Have your cartridges in the machines. Do be ready with your ad libs.

Avoid trying to get carts in the machines while you are talking on mike.

21. Do stay on top of the weather forecast and current market conditions.

22. Do sell PSA spots.

23. Do promo other jocks. Sell the DJs, sell the station. Use the call letters for everything.

24. Do check the bulletin board daily for special or regular assignments.

25. Do complete your assignments on time.

26. Do fill in your time sheet on time. And be sure to sign your real name, not your air name.

27. Do get involved in the community.

28. Do get involved in your station. Take an interest in something besides your air show.

Production

9

I firmly believe that good production men are born, not made. A good production man is a combination announcer, writer, engineer, musician, inventor, clairvoyant, salesman, and memory expert. He is all these things because he must be able to announce, write copy, run the board, know music, create new sounds and recording methods, save sounds and music he might be able to use in the future, and sell his finished product to a client, salesman, or program director. He must also be able to remember where every cymbal, beep, drum roll, fanfare, stinger, riff, or musical bridge ever recorded is located. Not every announcer can be a great production man. They are a breed all by themselves. But every announcer can improve his production technique and become more than adequate.

The only way to learn production is by constant experimentation in the production studio. You can read a book on how to improve your golf game, but to actually realize any improvement you must get out on the course. The same is true for production. The art of production cannot be taught, or I should say learned, with a book. Expertise in production is a feel, an ear, a sixth sense of what you are doing. However, I can present some basic production techniques to help you do a better job. To become good, get into the production studio and experiment. I can tell you how to make a splice, but you have to get into the studio and "feel" the splice. I can tell you to put a stinger after this word, but you have to get into the studio to "feel" what type of stinger to use. I can tell you that the "voice" has to be just right for each commercial, but you have to get into the studio to "feel" that voice. Production is the art of feeling with your ear. We can cover only the basics of that art.

WRITING FOR PRODUCTION

Defined, production is the transfer of words (copy) into sound, to become the tangible result of an idea. It is the art of creating audio pictures by combining sounds and words.

For many years the production of commercials and spot announcements consisted primarily of adding music to the words. This was considered a production spot. Then one day a salesman advised a copywriter that the client wanted an attention getter at the beginning of the commercial, and so a clanging bell was introduced into the commercial and the "loud" commercial was born. Bells clanging, sirens wailing, horns honking, buzzers buzzing, brakes squealing, and glass breaking—these were the production aids of radio in the late 50s. For several years radio did its very best to burst the eardrums of the listeners.

Finally, good sense and creativity prevailed. Copywriters, salesmen, and announcers found that commercials and announcements could be much more effective if the sounds added to a spot blended, rather than contrasted, with the words or message. It was discovered that moods could be created, pictures painted, and ideas and themes punctuated with the creative and proper use of music, sounds, and sound effects.

Writing commercial copy required a totally new concept. Sounds could either reenforce or replace words. And that, basically, is the reason for writing a production spot. You write to allow a sound, or sounds, do the work of words or to reenforce the words used. The utilization of sounds in an announcement means the message is more palatable to the listener's ear and, with the right sounds, the listener is literally forced to become involved by using his own imagination to decipher the sounds.

In writing a straight piece of copy, you generally allow approximately 150 to 160 words per minute. In writing production copy, for every one second of isolated sound you need six less words of copy. So, in a one-minute spot announcement, if you have ten seconds of isolated sound this means you should have approximately 60 less words in your copy. The remaining 90 have to be totally pertinent to the message or idea. No extra or unnecessary words can be tolerated. Incidentally, by isolated sound I refer to the use of a sound or sound effect without the announcer talking over it, a sound which is distinctively separate from the words of the copy.

In writing production copy, it is important to remain well within the range of your available talent and production aids. For example, you may have a tremendous idea for a commercial, utilizing a Scotch accent and bagpipes. However, your production library may be fresh out of bagpipes and everyone on the staff thinks a Scotch accent comes out of a bottle. My suggestion is to not get hung up on an idea if the necessary ingredients are not readily available. Rather than produce a poor spot with what you have available, use another idea. Remember that potentially good commercials are ruined with an unsuitable voice. Work with and around what you have.

When you write straight copy, your sentences can ramble on and on and on. In production copy, the sentences must be crisp, short, and to the point, especially if two or more voices are used. Everytime an announcer stops to take a breath, a second is lost. Breathe five times in a 60-second spot and you suddenly have a 55-second spot. Also, if the sentences are crisp and short, the spot will move and flow. Otherwise, the spot will drag. For example, get a partner and read the following exercises:

1ST: THE FOURTH ANNUAL FORD ROUNDUP SALE IS NOW UNDERWAY AT JOHNSON FORD, ON THE CORNER OF ELK AND MAIN STREETS IN DOWNTOWN. ALL NEW FORDS HAVE BEEN REDUCED AND THIS IS THE TIME TO BUY IF YOU REALLY WANT TO SAVE MONEY.

2ND: DURING THIS FOURTH ANNUAL ROUNDUP SALE YOU CAN SAVE UP TO TWO HUNDRED DOLLARS ON EVERY NEW PINTO FORD. UP TO FIVE HUNDRED DOLLARS ON A NEW LTD FORD. AND UP TO SIX HUNDRED DOLLARS ON A NEW DEMONSTRATOR.

Now, we'll take the same spot, same words, and write for a production spot.

> 1ST: THE FOURTH ANNUAL FORD ROUNDUP SALE IS NOW UNDERWAY!
> 2ND: AT JOHNSON FORD, ON THE CORNER OF ELK AND MAIN STREETS, DOWNTOWN.
> 1ST: ALL NEW FORDS HAVE BEEN REDUCED,
> 2ND: AND THIS IS THE TIME TO BUY IF YOU WANT TO REALLY SAVE MONEY.
> 1ST: DURING THIS FOURTH ANNUAL ROUNDUP SALE YOU CAN SAVE UP TO TWO HUNDRED DOLLARS ON EVERY NEW PINTO FORD.
> 2ND: UP TO FIVE HUNDRED DOLLARS ON A NEW LTD FORD,
> 1ST: AND UP TO SIX HUNDRED DOLLARS ON A NEW DEMONSTRATOR.

Get the picture? The shorter, more crisp the sentence, the more the spot moves. Use short phrases and word groupings, not long thoughts and sentences.

In Chapter 6, under the commercial classifications, I gave an example of the audio picture. Here is another audio picture which virtually eliminates the need to write, other than to have a few words to set the scene.

> ANNCR: A LOT OF PEOPLE HAVE THE MISTAKEN IDEA THAT MOBILE HOMES ARE TOO SMALL. LET'S WALK THROUGH A MOBILE HOME.
> SOUND EFFECT: (45 SECONDS OF FOOTSTEPS)
> ANNCR: GET THE PICTURE. ABC MOBILE HOMES, HIGHWAY 21 NORTH.

If you can put your hands on a sound effects record with footsteps, listen to 45 seconds of someone walking. It's almost an eternity. Here, we've let the sound do the work of the words.

In fact, all the words in the world could not have portrayed a picture as vividly as 45 seconds of sound effect. Let the sound work for you.

In a piece of straight copy you need only to concentrate on the proper selection and arranging of words. In a piece of production copy, you need to concentrate on the proper selection and arranging of the words and the proper selection and arranging of the sounds and music.

MUSIC AS A PRODUCTION AID

Far too often, music is added to a commercial just because "We always put music behind the commercial." Well, it is not always necessary to have music behind a spot. And in many cases the music may actually detract from the message. If you feel you need music, be careful in your selection.

In selecting music, avoid using tunes or melodies that are familiar. Very few stations have an adequate music library, so it is only natural to turn to albums for production music. However, I would suggest that you do not overlook new singles. Record companies constantly release instrumentals which always seem to get lost or buried in the station library. Have your music director save all instrumental single releases for possible use in the production studio.

After you have selected your music, make sure the record is not scratchy. Many a good idea has been ruined with the use of scratchy records. If the record is the least bit worn, get rid of it. When you've finished with the record, put the date on the album cut or record label. This will help prevent using the same piece of music for another sponsor. If you fail to date the selection, chances are you will end up with three or four commercials on the air with identical musical backgrounds.

Select music which will blend with your station format. If you have a Top 40 format, you certainly do not want to use the Guy Lombardo orchestra for a musical background. By the same token, if you are a M-O-R station, you will want to avoid the hard rock instrumentals.

As you audition album cuts and singles, try to store away in your mind the location of selections you may want to use later. You may even want to start a card file for various type cuts. For example, if you hear a good drum roll which might be of use at a later date, make an entry on a card. I would suggest using a ruler to actually measure the point where the

SOUND EFFECTS FILE CARD

DRUM ROLL

1. Hugo Winterhalter Plays   Side B Cut 4   9/16"
   The Hits

drum roll is located. (See the illustration.) Translated, your card tells you there is a drum roll on the album, "Hugo Winterhalter Plays The Hits." The drum roll is on side B, Cut 4, and is nine-sixteenths of inch into the cut. The measurement helps you to avoid wasting time looking for a 2-second drum roll. I would suggest an alphabetical card file, with a card for every imaginable sound and sound effect you might discover on albums (categories such as flutes, strings, fanfares, harp, etc.). This will save you a lot of time at a later date.

However, most good production men will record, immediately, anything they discover on an album. By recording, they have a permanent sound library which can be used over and over again without the fear of scratchiness. If you do record the sound, I would suggest a recording at 15 and 7½ IPS. Just as sure as you record at 15 (for quality), there will not be a playback unit for 15 at your next station and you will not be able to use your recorded sounds.

Musical punctuators are musical exclamation points. A punctuator is used within the spot to accent or stress an idea, word, or phrase. For example:

ANNCR: NOW AT JOHNSON FORD, THE FOURTH ANNUAL ROUNDUP SALE WITH SAVINGS ON EVERY NEW CAR ON THE LOT.
SOUND EFFECT: PUNCTUATOR — Side B Cut 1 — Basie Swings
ANNCR: SAVE UP TO ONE HUNDRED DOLLARS ON.....

The musical punctuator helps emphasize "savings on every new car on the lot" or separates the two thoughts. **Stinger** is just another word for "musical ending" and it is exactly that. Stinger signals the end of a commercial. A fanfare is a "musical beginning" and it signals the start of a commercial. For those reasons, I've always avoided using fanfares and stingers. With the recent concept of clustering commercials, a stinger merely gets in the way in the cluster, unless it is very, very, very quick. The fanfare has become a tune-out factor because it telegraphs the approach of a commercial and the listener's attention drifts away. You will have to exercise your own discretion in the use of these two musical aids. Music can be an invaluable production aid, but use it wisely.

SOUND EFFECTS

Sound effects are to a production man what colors are to an artist. Too much, and reality or believability is lost. Too little and you create a void or incompleteness.

Sound effects are used in many ways; however, the most common usage is to replace or reenforce words in your copy. For example:

(A) **Original sentence in copy reads:**

IN THE SPRING, A YOUNG MAN'S FANCY TURNS TO LOVE.

(B) **Sentence with sounds used to reenforce words.**

SOUND EFFECT: BIRDS CHIRPING

ANNCR: IN THE SPRING, A YOUNG MAN'S FANCY TURNS TO LOVE......

(C) **Sentence with sounds used as substitute for words.**

SOUND EFFECT: BIRDS CHIRPING....

ANNCR: THAT TIME OF YEAR AGAIN, WHEN A YOUNG MAN'S FANCY TURNS TO LOVE.....

In example A, we have the straight copy without the benefit of sound effects. Then, in B we reenforced the words with a sound associated with Spring—the birds chirping. And in C we eliminate the word Spring, substitute the birds, and by saying, "That time of the year again," we force the listener to think of Spring.

We could even get more effect by using a double reenforcement:

SOUND EFFECT: BIRDS CHIRPING. MUSIC — FADE OVER BIRDS AND DOWN SLOWLY FOR:

ANNCR: THAT TIME OF YEAR WHEN A YOUNG MAN'S FANCY TURNS TO LOVE...

In the example we have added music (something appropriate which would denote Spring) and now have a sound reenforcing the reenforcement, or, in other words, a double reenforcement. It is even possible to have a triple reenforcement:

SOUND EFFECT: BIRDS CHIRPING, WATER RUSHING BY (STREAM OR BROOK). MUSIC — FADE IN AND DOWN FOR:

ANNCR: THAT TIME OF YEAR WHEN A YOUNG MAN'S FANCY TURNS TO LOVE....

I would suggest that the triple reenforcement be used very sparingly. Too much clutter can't possibly help get your message across.

Sound effects, used properly, can be your most valuable production aid. The right sound effect will do many things:

1. Enable the production man to establish immediate product identification:

SOUND EFFECT: ELECTRIC TYPEWRITER

ANNCR: TYPEWRITERS ARE OUR BUSINESS AT.....

2. Enable the production man to create a mood:

SOUND EFFECT: RESTAURANT SOUNDS (PEOPLE TALKING — SOFT BACKGROUND PIANO) — FADE DOWN FOR:

ANNCR: IF YOU ARE LOOKING FOR A PLACE TO RELAX,

3. Enables the production man to establish a point or situation very quickly, even to the point of eliminating words:

SOUND EFFECTS: BREAKING GLASS (ONE SECOND PAUSE). TELEPHONE IS PICKED UP AND DIALED. TELEPHONE RINGS TWICE. TELEPHONE PICKED UP:

ANNCR: ATLAS GLASS REPAIR?

There is actually no limit to what you can accomplish with the proper sound effect, possibly because you have two great things going for you: the human ear and human imagination. For your commercials to be a success, do not abuse either.

JINGLES AS A PRODUCTION AID

The first jingles I remember hearing on a radio station were the Virginia Dare and Pepsi Cola commercials. Everyone remembers them because they were the only ones. Today, I can't recall more than a half dozen jingles presently in use. The jingle is probably the most overused production aid we have. Every client, from the moment he begins to advertise, envisions his own jingle extolling the merits of his company. Consequently, in my opinion, jingles have reached the saturation point and have lost their effectiveness—unless a client's advertising budget is large enough to insure a complete blitz of the airwaves. With enough money spent on advertising, a jingle can be effective. Otherwise, the jingle tends to get lost in the shuffle. The success of Winston Cigarettes, Coca Cola, and a few other jingles was due in part to the tremendous amount of advertising money expended to back up the jingle.

I assume that by now you have guessed I am not totally in favor of jingles as a production aid. You are right. Where possible, I avoid using a jingle because I feel they have lost the ability to be effective or sell. If it ever becomes absolutely necessary (due to a client's insistence) to use a jingle, try to use the jingle as a tag-out on your commercial message. It can't do any harm, there at the end, and will serve as a beautiful out-cue for the announcer running the board.

Jingles are really image builders and the effectiveness of a jingle is directly proportional to the frequency of use. So, if your client has a lot of money, a jingle, and wants to build an image, by all means use his jingle. On the other hand, if he wants to sell merchandise, use a production spot. To me, jingles are a no-no.

EDITING AND SPLICING

Rarely will you produce a commercial that does not need a little editing before you have a completed spot. You may need to tighten up a spot (delete a breath or dead area)or take out a word. Therefore, to become a good production man it is mandatory you become proficient with a splicer or splicing bar.

Most professional studios today use the splicing bar, which is a small tape-size bar on the tape recorder. I'm very much like an old dog who can't learn new tricks, and have always used a regular splicing machine. My particular favorite is the heavy-duty "Gibson Girl" manufactured by Robbias Electrical Corp.

What is editing? It is the rearranging of a piece of copy or music by either deleting from or adding to the recording tape with a splicing bar or machine. Splicing or editing is an art and cannot be learned from a book. The only way to master this art is to get into the production studio and practice. However, the following illustrations will give you the basic idea:

1. We will record this sentence, THE QUICK BROWN FOX JUMPED OVER THE LAZY DOG. If we could see the words on the tape, they would look like this:

GOD YZAL EHT REVO DEPMUJ XOF
NWORB KCIUQ EHT

What we want to do is delete the word **brown** from the sentence. On most tape machines there are three heads. From left to right the first head is the **erase head**, the second or middle head is the **recording** head, and the third head is the **playback** head.

Cue the tape up to the very beginning of the sentence on the tape machine. Now, press the start button. When the tape reaches the end of the word **quick**, stop the tape. With your hands, move the two reels of the tape machine from the left to the right, or vice versa, backwards or forwards, until the K of quick is resting right on top of the playback head (B). If you could read the words on the recording tape, they would appear as shown in the illustration. We are now ready to make the first edit mark. With a white grease pencil, make a small dot on the tape right where the "K" ends (C). Now, move the tape very slowly forward until you can hear the beginning of the word **fox**. When the f is resting on the playback head, stop and make another mark with your grease pencil (D). Lift the tape from the tape machine. The recording tape should have two edit marks (E) on it.

Now, place the first edit mark on top of the diagonal slash on the splicing bar of your splicing machine. Make a cut. Move the second edit mark to the top of the diagonal slash on the splicing bar and make another cut. The two pieces of tape will look like drawing F in the illustration. Bring the two ends together, place them in the splicing bar end to end, apply a small piece of splicing tape and press it on firmly. Use the splicer to trim the edges, remove the tape from the splicer and your edit is completed. If you could read the words on the tape, the word **brown** would be missing (G).

That's all there is to editing. As you become proficient in the art of editing and splicing, you will find that you'll be able to edit out a syllable in a word or a tinkle of a bell in a musical piece. You will be limited only by your ability. And your ability will depend entirely on the amount of practice you have.

Tape Editing & Splicing Procedure

A ☐ ☐ ☐
ERASE RECORD PLAYBACK
TYPICAL TAPE HEAD LAYOUT

B GOD YZAL EHT REVO DEPMUJ XOF NWORB KCIUQ EHT
ERASE RECORD PLAYBACK

C GOD YZAL EHT REVO DEPMUJ XOF NWORB•KCIUQ EHT

D GOD YZAL EHT REVO DEPMUJ XOF•NWORB KCIUQ EHT

E GOD YZAL EHT REVO DEPMUJ XOF•NWORB•KCIUQ EHT

F

SPLICING TAPE

G GOD YZAL EHT REVO DEPMUJ XOF KCIUQ EHT
(THE QUICK FOX JUMPED OVER THE LAZY DOG)

VOICE TRACK FILE

Earlier, we mentioned the importance of using good voices in your commercials, and I suggested that you contact the local drama clubs to obtain these voices. Once you have the people in your studio, you might consider recording the commercial twice. Once to be produced for the station, and the second time in order to acquire a master voice track bed. You can save the voice tracks and use them over and over again.

PRODUCTION TRICKS

The secret to production is the proper sound and the retention of those sounds. Listed below are some tips on how to acquire different sounds and how to become a better production man.

1. To speed up the sound of voice or music, wrap Scotch tape around the capstan of the tape machine. By experimenting you will know just how much tape to wrap around the capstan.

2. Variable-speed record players are now available and occasionally you may obtain an appropriate sound by speeding up or slowing down a record. If you do not have a variable-speed record player, try playing the record at various speeds (78 or 45).

3. The days of heavy echo have long since passed. However, just a tiny shade of echo on your commercials will give them presence and in most cases fill those empty spots with audio.

4. Get your engineer to show you how to "phase" a tape recorder and commercial. The eerie effect may be worth using.

5. Presence or depth may be added to a spot by the use of multi-recording, making two voices out of one.

6. When producing a commercial, sometimes the best results are obtained by producing it in segments rather than trying to accomplish the complete recording in one sitting. Record in segments, then splice the segments together.

7. Have your engineer install a filter mike. Sometimes the contrast in voice has an excellent effect. An old headset or telephone makes a workable filter mike.

8. Reverse echo, or where the echo moves from the rear to the front, rather than from front to the rear, is achieved in the following manner. Record the spot in the normal manner. Reverse the tape and play the spot backwards into another recording machine, adding echo. Now, rewind the tape to its original form and play back on the first machine. You have reverse echo.

9. To achieve a multivoice effect without dubbing from machine to machine, disconnect the erase head and just keep recording on top of a spot. This is easier to accomplish with a cartridge machine than a tape recorder because the cart will stop automatically at the beginning of the spot.

10. Always make masters on new tape. Never use the stretch-type tape, either. Use standard 1.5 mil broadcast tape.

11. Unusual musical sounds may be obtained by recording a piece of music and then playing the tape backwards. For even a more weird effect, put reverse echo on the music.

12. Whenever you get a call from a listener with an unusual voice such as a British accent or French accent, ask him or her to record several voice tracks for future use. Then save those voice tracks.

13. Never use any voice or voice track which has been copyrighted. For example, some production men obtain voice tracks from television cartoons. They may sound great, but it is illegal to use them and you will get into a little hot water. The same rule applies to commercials from agencies and to public service announcements. And do not lift anything from a music service library unless the station subscribes to the library service.

14. The quality of cassette machines today is such that every good production man should have one. With a light-weight cassette machine, you can record your own sound effects for possible use. Over a period of time you will build quite a library of sounds.

15. Remember, the more dubbing you do, the poorer the quality becomes. Avoid using second and third generation dubs. The quality is too poor.

16. Always keep a supply of head cleaner and a box of Q-Tips handy. Dirty recording heads have messed up many a spot. Keep your recording heads clean.

17. I always carry a small overnight bag with me whenever I'm going to do production. In the bag I keep (1) head cleaner, (2) several rolls of splicing tape, (3) several reels of leader tape, (4) several small reels of recording tape, (5) several blank reels of various sizes, (6) several reels of new or clean recording tape, (7) a stop-watch, (8) several grease pencils of various colors—black, red, white, (9) ballpoint pens, (10) labels, (11) yellow legal pads, (12) matches and a pack of cigarettes, and (13) jack cords for every possible situation. Everything I might possibly need is packed into the bag.

18. Always keep your master tapes of voice tracks and sound effects with you or in a safe place. Leave the tape(s) lying around and someone is going to grab it by mistake and erase it.

10 Ratings

Most people take one look at a rating book and cringe. At first glance, a rating book does appear to be extremely complicated. However, you do not have to own a master's degree in math to understand one. The following material should give you a basic understanding of how a ratings book is compiled, and how to read and understand the information contained in the book.

The three most often used rating services or audience measurement services are the American Research Bureau (ARB), C. E. Hooper, Inc., and The Pulse, Inc. The methods most commonly utilized to gather data are the telephone interview, the diary, and the personal interview.

The **telephone interview,** as the term suggests, is an interview conducted by telephone. This is generally referred to as a **coincidental review** and the respondent is asked to state which station he or she is listening to at the exact time the interview is being conducted or, in some cases, at the instant the respondent answered the telephone.

The **diary** is a type of questionnaire in which the respondent is asked to furnish a written record of behavior for a specified period of time. Almost all diaries are self-administered by the respondent in that the respondent must fill in the diary without assistance from an interviewer. There are several types of diaries. The individual diary is one that requires a record of behavior for a particular individual. The household diary requires a record of the behavior for all members of the family or household (sometimes referred to as the family diary). The closed-end diary lists specific time segments (15-minute intervals) for each broadcast day covered by a survey. The person keeping the diary is instructed to show, for each 15-minute period, whether a radio set is on or off. Whenever the set is on, they must indicate the station to which the set is dialed, the name of the program being broadcast, and who in the family or household is listening. The open-end diary does not list specific time segments. Rather, it consists of blank lines. The respondent is asked to record the time that he or she turns the radio on and begins to listen. When the set is on, the respondent has to list the station, name of program, and who in the household is listening.

The personal interview is a situation in which the person conducting the interview asks questions of the respondent in person at the respondent's residence.

These are the three basic methods of broadcast research. I will hasten to add that the methodology is a bit more complicated with many factors and variables included. However, at this time, we will stick to basics.

From the information received in the research method, an audience measurement firm is able to correlate the statistics and information and arrive at the following for each station in the market: (1) Share of audience estimates in-home and out-of-home, (2) Average ¼-hour ratings and shares, and (3) Cumulative audience estimates and demographic characteristics.

To enable you to understand how to read a "book," you first must understand the broadcast research terms used. Familiarize yourself with these terms:

Audience: A group of households or individuals that are counted in a radio audience. Audience measurements are usually expressed in two ways: as percentages (called ratings) and as absolute quantities (representing either a number of households or individuals).

Audience composition: Refers to a classification of the individuals or the households in a radio audience. Broken down into various categories such as age and sex groupings (men, women, teenagers, children).

Audience share: The percent of all listeners in a market that a particular station gets at a given time.

Average audience rating: The rating that is computed for some specified period of time (15 minute periods).

Audience survey: A market study that computes audience share and audience rating (ARB, Hooper, Pulse).

Coincidental survey: A telephone interview.

Cost per thousand: Not a rating term, but it is figured from the ratings. It is the ratio of the cost of radio advertisement in dollars to a number of individuals (in thousands) estimated to be in the audience at the time the commercial is broadcast.

Cume: The short for cumulative audience. See below.

Cumulative audience: Known more simply as cume. It is the total number of different listeners reached by a station in two or more time periods.

Demographics: The "who" of radio. Audience composition. Age, sex, etc.

Demographic characteristics: Refers to the various social and economic characteristics of a group of households or individuals.

Diary: Type of questionnaire utilized in a survey.

Gross rating points: The total of radio ratings during two or more time periods, or for two or more programs.

H.U.R.: Homes Using Radio. A type of rating which expresses the percentage of households that are estimated to be in the audience of any one of a group of radio stations at a specified time.

Metro rating: A rating computed for the households or individuals in a defined metropolitan area.

Metro share: A share, or share of audience percentage, computed for a defined metropolitan area.

Program rating: A rating that shows the percentage of radio households or a group of individuals that is estimated to be in a program's audience during a specified period.

Rating: The size of a radio audience expressed in relative or percentage terms.

Share of audience: The percentage of the radio audience in some specified area at a specified time. Simply called "share."

Station rating: Any rating computed for a radio station. This kind of rating shows the percentage of radio households or individuals among those in a specified area which is estimated to be a station's audience over a specified period of time.

Total audience rating: A rating computed for some specified period of time (15 minutes). To be counted in the audience, a person or household must have listened for five consecutive minutes or more.

Turnover: The ratio of a cumulative audience over several different periods of time to the average audience per period of time. This ratio provides an indication of the relative frequency with which the audience of a program or station changes during a period of time.

READING A RATING BOOK

We will now look at a typical metropolitan market survey book. The illustrations and market information were obtained from an actual survey and provided by Pulse. Inc. Only portions of the survey were selected as illustrations and in some cases do not reflect total time periods and are presented incomplete.

SPECIFIC INFORMATION ABOUT THE SURVEY MARKET

Sample Size

The total number of roster re-call interviews for the survey: 381

Number used in survey: 373

Number unusable interviews: 8

Not-at-home contacts: 233

Refusals: 113

Base for ratings

Base used for computation of the average ¼-hour ratings was 373

Persons reached estimates

The base for computing the persons reached ratings are applicable to the day parts, and the estimated population for a projection of these ratings are shown below:

AGE	ESTIMATED POPULATION		MONDAY-FRIDAY BASE	
	MEN (00)	WOMEN (00)	MEN	WOMEN
18-24	153	146	26	39
25-34	154	155	45	56
35-49	194	202	67	105
50-64	119	137	55	69
65 & over	61	84	26	41
TOTAL	681	724	219	310
Teens (12 - 17)	221		83	
Children (4 - 11)	318		7	

Respondents & Absentees

At the time the interview was conducted the following members of the household were:

	PRESENT	ABSENT
Men (18 & over)	219	124
Women (18 & over)	310	96
Teens (12 - 17)	83	50
Children (4 - 11)	7	132

Loosely translated, the preceding information advises us that a total of 381 interviews were conducted. Of the 381, 8 were thrown out for some reason and the actual number used was 373. The base for computing the persons ratings is taken from the respondents and absentees column. Notice the totals for men and women in the Monday-Friday (base) period. They correspond. The 310 women and 219 men are further broken down into specific age groups. The figures to the left (estimated population) were obtained from a particular source and represent the population of the market. From these figures and the firm's records, the following ratings were computed.

Illustration A shows the share of audience estimates. The share of audience is generally the percentage of the entire radio audience in a specified area at a specified time which makes up the audience of a station. A share may be computed either on a household or individual basis. In this particular illustration we see the percentages expressed in homes and individuals (men, women, teens, and total). The figures expressed do not represent **actual** homes or individuals but **estimated** homes and individuals. You will notice that in the teens column, the shares add to more than 100 percent, while in the other columns the shares add to less than 100 percent. The shares of stations in a given market may sum to more than 100 percent because some households or individuals may be counted in the audience of two or more stations during a specified period of time. Or, hese shares may sum to less than 100 percent because some households or individuals may be counted in the audiences of stations that are outside of the market or otherwise not reported.

In this illustration Station D and Station F clearly dominate the market in all categories, except that station F has virtually no teens in its audience between 6 AM and midnight.

The small letter "a" which appears after certain figures is a notation that the station does not broadcast for the complete period (6 AM - midnight) due to limited broadcast hours and-or AM-FM duplication. The blanks indicate less than ½ of one percent. Therefore, no figure may be given as it would be too small.

Illustration B shows the average ¼-hour audience estimates. This is a type of rating computed for a specified interval of time, in this case ¼-hour segments. The audience measurements are estimates of audience size. The rating

A

<u>THE PULSE, INC.</u>

SHARE OF AUDIENCE ESTIMATES

<u>(CITY)</u>   METROPOLITAN AREA

| STATIONS | MONDAY – FRIDAY | |
	HOMES %	MEN %
A	3	
B	3A	4A
C	2A	1A
D	28	35
E	5A	8A
F	33	22
FF	2A	3A
G	9	7
H	9	9
I	4A	4A
TRP	18.0	
PUR IN 100's		89

*TOTAL INCLUDES CHILDREN

OCT. - NOV., 1969

6:00 A.M. - MIDNIGHT

WOMEN %	TEENS %	TOTAL* %
3		1
3A	A	3A
1A	A	1A
17	74	34
7A	6A	7A
42	3	26
1A	A	2A
9		7
10	18	12
3A	3A	4A
88	34	219

B

THE PULSE, INC.

AVERAGE ¼ HOUR AUDIENCE ESTIMATES

___(CITY)___ METROPOLITAN AREA MONDAY

6 A.M. - 10 A.M.
PERSONS REACHES ESTIMATES

STA.	AVG ¼ HR RATING	MEN (00)	WOMEN (00)	TEENS (00)	CHILD (00)	TOTAL (00)	MEN 18-24 (00)
A	.2	1	1			2	
B	.1		1			1	
C	.8	3	4			7	
D	6.1	41	24	20	11	96	12
E	1.7	9	13	2		24	2
F	12.2	38	81	1		120	1
FF							
G	2.4	12	13			25	3
H	1.0	6	5	2		13	5
I	.5	2	2			4	
MISC	.8						
TOTAL	25.6	115	145	25	11	296	23

Persons Reached Estimates by Age

MEN 25-34 (00)	MEN 35-49 (00)	MEN 50-64 (00)	WOMEN 18-24 (00)	WOMEN 25-34 (00)	WOMEN 35-49 (00)	WOMEN 50-64 (00)
1						
					1	
1		1		3		
17	10	2	9	7	7	1
	5	1		1	5	7
9	14	13	7	20	19	23
1	4	2			3	3
			1	3	1	
1	1			1	1	
30	36	20	17	35	37	35

C

THE PULSE, INC.

AVERAGE ¼ HOUR AUDIENCE

(CITY)	METROPOLITAN AREA		MONDAY

STA.	6:00A.M. Avg. ¼ Hr Rating	6:30A.M. Avg. ¼ Hr Rating	7:00A.M. Avg. ¼ Hr Rating	7:30A.M. Avg. ¼ Hr Rating
A				.3
B				
C			1.2	1.2
D	3.5	5.3	10.3	9.9
E	3.6	4.4	3.0	1.0
F	7.5	10.0	17.2	16.0
FF				
G	.7	.7	2.4	2.8
H	.7	.5	1.4	1.1
I		.6	.5	.7
Misc		.2	.6	1.3
TOTAL	16.0	21.2	36.0	34.3

ESTIMATES - In-Home & Out-of-Home

- Friday   Oct - Nov, 1969

8:00A.M. Avg. ¼ Hr Rating	8:30A.M. Avg. ¼ Hr Rating	9:00A.M. Avg. ¼ Hr Rating	9:30A.M. Avg. ¼ Hr Rating	10:00A.M. Avg. ¼ Hr Rating
.6	.4	.2	.2	.6
		.4	.4	.6
1.1	1.1	.6	.4	.4
7.9	4.7	3.7	3.5	3.0
.7	.5	.2	.2	.2
15.3	11.4	9.1	10.7	9.8
3.5	3.1	3.1	3.1	1.7
1.2	1.0	1.0	1.1	1.2
.8	.8	1.0	1.0	1.8
.8	.8	1.0	1.0	.8
31.3	23.2	20.1	21.4	19.3

D

<u>The Pulse, Inc.</u>

CUMULATIVE AUDIENCE ESTIMATES

<u>(city)</u>   Metropolitan Area

STA.	M - F Daily (00)	Mon. - Sun. 24 Hours Persons Reached Estimates					
		Homes (00)	Men (00)	Women (00)	Teens (00)	Total* (00)	Men 18-24 (00)
A	17	35	27	35	2	64	
B	8	14	21	13		34	13
C	10	13	13	15		27	
D	198	303	313	291	179	873	100
E	53	101	141	189	28	357	46
F	272	351	309	378	26	713	25
FF	17	50	57	35	2	94	21
G	67	96	88	71	4	164	17
H	59	138	190	134	110	478	101
I	28	52	66	35	9	109	13
All Sta	484	563	625	666	217	1643	153

*Total Includes Children

OCT -- NOV, 1969

PERSONS REACHED ESTIMATES BY AGE

MEN 25-34 (00)	MEN 35-49 (00)	MEN 50-64 (00)	WOMEN 18-24 (00)	WOMEN 25-34 (00)	WOMEN 35-49 (00)	WOMEN 50-64 (00)
9	16	2		15	7	9
6		2	2	4	5	2
9		2		9	2	1
86	81	33	83	75	78	37
7	50	24	45	26	54	41
77	88	86	40	75	104	98
15	13	8	4	4	16	5
20	30	12		4	23	21
21	42	14	30	44	33	13
33	14	6	5	15	15	
154	171	106	129	146	191	124

E

The Pulse, Inc.

CUMULATIVE AUDIENCE ESTIMATES

| (CITY) | METROPOLITAN AREA | | | | | MONDAY |

| STATIONS | 6 A.M. - 10 A.M. PERSONS REACHED ESTIMATES | | | | | |
	HOMES (00)	MEN (00)	WOMEN (00)	TEENS (00)	*TOTAL (00)	MEN 18-24 (00)
A	22	19	17		36	
B	6	11	2		14	8
C	11	10	10		19	
D	197	193	172	136	546	71
E	74	95	111	14	220	36
F	284	213	308	18	540	4
FF						
G	61	65	43		107	8
H	78	68	66	86	220	40
I	32	30	26	4	60	4
ALL STA	512	535	566	173	1319	128

*TOTAL INCLUDES CHILDREN

Persons Reached Estimates by Age						
Men 25-34 (00)	Men 35-49 (00)	Men 50-64 (00)	Women 18-24 (00)	Women 25-34 (00)	Women 35-49 (00)	Women 50-64 (00)
9	10			7	2	7
3					2	
6		2		4	2	1
57	47	16	56	50	49	11
	38	14	10	12	39	33
59	62	75	24	60	89	82
20	23	9		2	15	6
9	16		15	21	24	
15	6	5	5	11	10	
131	145	99	97	120	169	114

F

<u>The Pulse, Inc.</u>

CUMULATIVE AUDIENCE ESTIMATES

___(city)___ METROPOLITAN AREA MONDAY –

DRIVE TIMES 6 A.M. – 10 A.M. & 3 P.M. –– 7 P.M.
PERSONS REACHED ESTIMATES

STATIONS	HOMES (00)	MEN (00)	WOMEN (00)	TEENS (00)	*TOTAL (00)	MEN 18-24 (00)
A	28	21	26		47	
B	11	16	8		25	13
C	11	13	10		22	
D	249	259	217	174	740	88
E	84	124	134	26	283	46
F	723	180	230	20	549	13
FF	17	22	13	2	37	4
G	81	77	60	2	139	17
H	100	116	86	93	341	75
I	43	43	32	7	81	4
ALL STA	537	609	622	207	1574	153

*TOTAL INCLUDES CHILDREN

- In-Home & Out-of-Home

Friday   Oct - Nov, 1969

			Persons Reached Estimates by Age			
Men 25-34 (00)	Men 35-49 (00)	Men 50-64 (00)	Women 18-24 (00)	Women 25-34 (00)	Women 35-49 (00)	Women 50-64 (00)
9	12			13	5	7
3			2	2	3	1
9		2		4	2	1
72	63	25	71	60	65	15
7	50	14	26	12	46	33
72	3	75	31	68	96	22
9	3	6	4	2	3	4
20	23	10		4	19	15
15	23		25	25	24	6
24	10	5	5	15	12	
154	166	100	119	134	185	115

gives the average ¼-hour rating of the total audience listening to each station as the percentage of all homes interviewed. The average ¼-hour rating is shown in tenths in order to differentiate from shares which are shown in whole percentage points. This illustration reflects the average ¼-hour audience estimates for specific periods of time, in this case from 6 AM-10AM. Illustration C gives an hour-by-hour breakdown.

Illustration D reflects the cumulative audience estimates and a report of the circulation (number of listeners for a station) for a full week. This represents unduplicated listeners. The data is broken down into two categories: the persons reached estimates for Monday through Sunday and the persons reached estimates by age. This is probably the most important segment of any survey because it indicates who is listening to a particular station.

Illustration E is a further breakdown of the cumulative audience estimates by specific periods, in this case 6AM-10AM. And Illustration F is merely a combination of the cumulative audience for drive times (6AM-10AM and 3PM-7PM). The two have been added together to produce one report.

WHAT DO THE RATINGS TELL?

Years ago, about all that a rating revealed was which was the most popular or most listened to station in the market. Now, ratings tell you which station is the most listened to by a particular age group. Why is this important? The information allows a time buyer to make a more scientific decision on which stations to buy for a particular client.

Let's say that a client manufactures a pain reliever for arthritis and he wants to advertise his product in a market. This is a product of interest primarily to people in the 50-64 age bracket (an assumption). Refer to the cumulative audience estimates (D, E and F). A quick glance would indicate that the station to buy would be Station F, because it has almost three times as many listeners in that age bracket as the closest stations (Station D and Station E). The survey enables the time buyer to make a more informed decision on which stations to buy for various products and clients.

Programmers also use the ratings to analyze their station's weaknesses and strengths.

There are many who do not believe the ratings actually tell the true story. It's been my experience that this generally comes from the people who are low in the ratings. Basically, ratings are the yardstick by which a station's performance in a given market is measured. And you can believe them.

11 Making the Job Easier

At this point it is appropriate to consider a few suggestions, ideas, and pointers which should make your job a little easier and possibly more pleasant. Your life in radio can become most unpleasant if you can't get along with management and if you fail to observe FCC Rules.

BETTER RELATIONS WITH THE BOSS

Sometimes the art of "handling" the boss requires just as much work as programming the radio station. And in defense of general managers, sometimes the job of "handling" the program director requires just as much effort.

It is important that you understand that it is imperative that the general manager be surrounded by people who are "tuned to his frequency." A general manager, believe it or not, has enough problems without having to live with bad vibrations from members of his staff. Therefore, as the program director, it is your job to get along with the general manager. Your job depends on your ability to do so. Of course, everyone has little idiosyncrasies that irritate others, but for the most part we ignore them. Not so when it comes to the GM. We expect him to be perfect and sometimes more than human. Doesn't really make much sense does it? Take my advice. Learn your general manager's little quirks and learn to live with them.

Getting along with the boss might be particularly difficult if the man in question has never been a disc jockey or a program director. The ideal situation, as far as any program director is concerned, is to have a boss who came up through the ranks, so to speak. However, as most of us know, many managers got their position for being the best salesman on the staff. And rightly so. They've earned it! However, this does not alter the fact that a "sales only" oriented general manager doesn't always have the most sympathetic ear when it comes to the programming department.

Let me suggest that you take advantage of the situation. If your general manager is a salesman, you can get and do anything you want, within reason, because the easiest man to sell is a salesman. So learn to sell. Forget about asking, pleading, demanding, begging, fighting, or complaining. Learn to sell. Read a few books on salesmanship. In fact, every program director and disc jockey should read a book or two on salesmanship. Who knows? Your sales technique might become so effective that you'll suddenly find yourself occupying a general manager's chair.

There is one very important thing to remember, if you want to enjoy excellent relations with your boss. A program director is a department head **under** the general manager. You must understand that, as program director, your loyalty belongs to the GM. Don't fight with him. Fight for him.

AIR CHECK FILE

As you make your weekly air checks, I suggest that you retain the good ones. It is not uncommon for someone to get fired in this business without any warning. And if the axe does fall you will at least have a decent air check. And, too, you never know when you're going to get a call from "Mr. Big" requesting an air check. If you have a good one in your file, then you won't have to worry about sneaking into the studios in the wee hours of the morning to produce one. And, of course, with an air check file you have an opportunity to keep an audio record of how well you are progressing from year to year, or even month to month.

GOLDEN RECORD REFERENCE BOOK

Our memories are not infallible, so try to talk your general manager into obtaining a copy of Joel Whitburn's Record Research Book. His address is 8447 Lloyd, Menomonee Falls, Wisc. 53051. Joel has compiled an alphabetical listing (by artist) of every song that has appeared on the Billboard Hot 100 since 1955. Listed under the artist's name is every record he ever cut, the date the record hit its highest ranking on the chart, the record's highest position, and the number of weeks the record was on the chart. The book is an invaluable tool for programmers and record librarians.

COMEDY MATERIAL

The following are sources of comedy and ad lib material for disc jockeys:

Contemporary Comedy
726 Chestnut Street
Suite "B"
Philadelphia, Pa. 19106

Laugh Service For Disc Jockeys
P.O. Box 612
Turnersville, New Jersey 08012

Orben's Current Comedy
1529 East 19th Street
Brooklyn, N.Y. 11230

Edmun Orrin
8034 Gentry Ave.
No. Hollywood, Calif. 91605

Quips, Quibbles, & Quotables
632 Geary Street
Harrisburg, Pa. 17110

Bob Raleigh's Weekly Comedy Service
P.O.Box 684
Galax, Virginia 24333

IN CASE OF FIRE

I doubt if one station in a hundred has an "In Case Of Fire" policy posted on the bulletin board. Hopefully, your station will never be so victimized, but just in case a fire does occur, I would suggest that you have your people briefed on what to do. Naturally, they are to seek their own safety. However, if there is time for them to save anything, tell them to save the commercials, the start order book, and the accounts receivable book. These are the most important items in a radio station. However, whenever a fire does occur, the staff invariably tries to save the record rack, the cartridge machines, the memos on the bulletin board. Remind them that insurance will replace the equipment, but nothing will replace your start order book or the accounts receivable records. And by saving the commercials also, you can be back on the air in a matter of hours (with borrowed equipment) without having to spend hours in a make-shift production studio reproducing commercials.

POLICY MANUAL

Every station should have a policy manual. If your station doesn't have one, make it your personal pet project. A policy manual is invaluable for indoctrinating new personnel and as a refresher for old personnel. It's just a good idea to have the station do's and don'ts set down in a permanent record.

And do you have an indoctrination policy? Most stations will hire a man, shake his hand, and point him in the general direction of the control room. Why not have a standard indoctrination period for a new employee. Explain all the programming policies and be sure to explain to him the policies regarding overtime, paydays, sick leave, vacation, time sheet procedures, talent and National Guard policy, if applicable.

SPEC TAPE SCORECARD

If you produce spec tapes for the sales department, keep a record of what is produced and what is sold. I generally use a sheet of graph paper and multicolored lines (bars) to indicate who produced what commercial for which salesman and the amount of the sale involved. At the end of the month, toot your horn a little. Send a memo to the general manager advising

Feb. Spec-Tape Scorecard

	AL-	Bob	John	Rich			Total Produced	Total Sold	$ Volume	
1	75.00 MARY TRESS	ARTHUR'S 700.00	CARRUTH	200.00 TONY'S					#	1
2	CARR MTRS 150.00 WILSON MTRS	MACY'S	HILL'S 150.00 THOMPSON	EDWARDS 200.00 JONES FURN			18	6	1175.00	2
3		MACY'S		WILSON MTRS						3
4	Johnson-									4
5	MACK'S CARPET			WEBB-						5
6				WILLIAMS						6
7				HI-LO						7
8										8
9										9
10										10

Sample graph showing tangible evidence of what the production department is doing in the way of generating new business. Each entry denotes that a commercial was cut for a client. Figures represent amount of money realized from the production of that commercial. In this graph, we see that a total of 18 commercials (spec-tapes) were produced in the month of February. Six were sold, by the sales department in the amount of $1175.00. Multiply this by 12 (months) and you have an excellent argument for a raise or request for more equipment.

him of what was accomplished in the production room that month.

If you keep a copy of each graph, it also makes a nice addition to your resume for that next job application. One thing any general manager is able to relate with immediately and that's sales. If your graphs are impressive, he'll be impressed.

MONTHLY PRODUCTION ANALYSIS

It's a good policy to keep track of how many commercials are produced during the month by each announcer. (See the accompanying illustration.) Again, report to the general manager, at the end of the month, advising him of how many pieces of production were handled by your department. This report not only reminds him of what a great job you're doing, but the figures will come in handy when you start talking about the necessity of adding another production man or a piece of equipment.

MARKET RESEARCH MATERIAL

Excellent research books containing valuable information about your market may be obtained for almost pennies. Write the Budget Division of the Department of Administration in your state and ask them to send you a copy of their County Profile. All states issue this little book, which is filled with facts and figures on your county and coverage area. For 25 cents each you may obtain two books from the U.S. Department of Commerce. Ask for "General Population Characteristics" and "General Housing Characteristics" for your state.

From the highway traffic department you should be able to obtain a "Traffic Flow Graph" for your city. This graph will show you where the peak traffic is located and at what time of the day. This graph may be used in many ways. At a glance you will be able to select the best locations for any billboards you plan to purchase and your morning and afternoon drive personalities will be able to determine when the peak automobile movement occurs. Also, the graph will give your

FEb - Production Analysis

	AL	Bob	John	Rich	MARK	Total Produced	PSA's
						97	13
	25	21	18	21	12		

As indicated, a total of 97 spots were produced. The check marks indicate or denote that the spot produced was a public service announcement. You could carry this graph a bit further by indicating the date the spot was cut.

sales department an excellent tool for selling night-time radio. The more you can find out about your market, the more adept you will be in programming for your market.

THE FEDERAL COMMUNICATIONS COMMISSION

Who originated the very first voice broadcast? Oldtimers and historians claim the honor belongs to Nathan B. Stubblefield who, in 1892, sent a voice message to his neighbor, Rainey T. Wells. The demonstration took place in Murray, Kentucky. There were other early experiments in voice broadcasting in the early 1900s, but it wasn't until after World War I that regularly scheduled broadcasting began.

KDKA, Pittsburgh has long been accepted as the "first" radio station in this country. However, the first license issued to a radio station went to WBZ in Springfield, Massachusetts (now WBZ Boston), on September 15, 1921. KDKA was not issued a license until November 7 of the same year (KDKA had been broadcasting as an experimental operation prior to that time).

The "network" was born in 1922 when WJZ in New York (now WABC) and WGY Schenectady broadcast the World Series. The first multistation hookup was initiated in 1922 when a subsidiary of RCA (NBC) started a network by joining 24 stations together for regular programming. Also, in the same year, The Columbia Phonograph Broadcasting System (now CBS) was organized. The third major network—ABC— was formed when the FCC ordered NBC to discontinue the operation of the Red and Blue networks. RCA sold the Blue network in 1943 and that was the beginning of ABC (American Broadcasting Co.).

Early broadcasting came under the regulation of the Secretary of Commerce. However, by 1926, radio had developed so rapidly that the Commerce Department was unable to deal with the problems being created. Radio broadcasters changed their frequencies, operating times, and power whenever they felt like it. Consequently, the airwaves were filled with confusion. Mass interference between station signals existed. Finally, in 1927, President Calvin Coolidge persuaded Congress to pass the Dill-White Radio Act. This bill created a 5-member "Federal Radio Commission" which was empowered to issue station licenses, allocate frequencies and control power. The same bill also gave the Secretary of Commerce authority to inspect radio stations and to assign radio call signs.

Then in 1934 President Roosevelt instructed the Secretary of Commerce to make a study of communications. Upon completion of the study, the Secretary recommended that Congress establish a single agency to regulate all communications by wire and radio. Congress accepted the recommendation and passed the "Communications Act of 1934," which created the Federal Communications Commission.

The FCC began operations on July 11, 1934 as an independent government agency headed by a 7-member commission. (Commissioners are appointed by the President, subject to the approval of Congress.) The main function of the FCC is the regulation of broadcasting which includes the allocation of frequencies, the assignment of stations to the frequencies, and the regulation of those stations by inspection and surveillance. Broadcast stations are licensed to serve in the public interest, and are licensed for a period of three years, at which time they must apply for renewal of that license.

Of course, we cannot go into all of the laws and regulations pertaining to the operation of a radio station. I do believe it behooves any operator (announcer) to be familiar with these rules and regulations and I would urge everyone in radio to obtain a copy of the Rules and Regulations and read them (every station has, or should have, a copy on file). Following is a discussion concerning the basic or most violated Rules and Regulations which apply directly to the announcer. Even if you have your operator's license, you should still be familiar with certain rules and regulations. So, I would suggest you commit the following to memory.

1. **Operator's license**: Any citizen may apply for a commercial license. Whenever a licensee qualifies for a higher grade of license, the original or lower-grade license is can-

celed upon issuance of the new license. If a license is lost, the Commission must be notified immediately and licensee must submit an application for a duplicate. A license is good or valid for five years and must be renewed upon expiration.

2. **Station log:** An announcer must sign the station log when starting duty and again when going off duty. The most common error among announcers is the failure to sign on and off the log. An error on the station log may be corrected only by the person originating the entry. That person should strike out the erroneous portion with a single line, initial the correction made, and indicate the date of the correction.

The following entries are to be made on the program log: (1) An entry of the time of each station identification announcement; (2) An entry briefly describing each program broadcast (such as music, sports, news, etc.) with the name of the program, sponsor's name (if any), and the beginning and ending time of the program. If a mechanical reproduction is used, an entry should show the exact nature such as "ET," "record," "tape," etc. If a speech is made by a political candidate, the name and political affiliation of the speaker must be entered; (3) An entry must be made showing that each sponsor has been announced; (4) An entry for each program of network origin. (Items 2 and 4 are generally pre-typed on the log and Item 3 usually needs only the announcer's check mark to signify that the listed commercial broadcast was identified as being commercial.) Station logs are retained by the station for a period of two years. Most stations retain logs for a period of five years. Logs should be kept in an orderly and legible manner. Each sheet must be numbered and dated and time entries shall be in local standard or daylight savings time (and must be so indicated). (For more information concerning logs see Sections 73.111 & 73.112 of the Rules and Regulations.

3. **Station identification:** It is necessary to broadcast a station identification announcement at the beginning and ending of each period of operation and regularly, during operation, within two minutes of each hour and each half hour. An official station ID (legal ID) consists of the station's call letters and name of the community specified in the

station's license. When given special authorization, a station may include in its official ID the name of an additional community; however, the community to which the station is licensed must be named first. The exact time of the ID must be noted on the program log. Failure to log station IDs is another of the more common errors committed by announcers. (For more details see Section 73.1201 of the Rules and Regulations.

4. **Suspension of a license:** A license may be suspended for damaging or permitting anyone to damage any radio equipment or facility, using false or deceptive signals or call letters and profane or obscene language, attempting to obtain (or being associated with an attempt to obtain) a license by fraudulent methods. There are many other grounds for license suspension, but these are the most pertinent to broadcasters.

5. **EBS:** The Emergency Broadcast System consists of radio stations and interconnecting facilities which have been authorized by the FCC to operate in a controlled manner upon notification. Notification can be given during war, threat of war, or state of emergency. (See Section 73.911 of the Rules and Regulations).

6. **EAC:** The Emergency Action Condition is the period which exists after the transmission of an Emergency Action Notification and before the transmission of the Emergency Action Termination. (Section 73.915) Every radio station has installed, unless otherwise exempt, the necessary equipment to receive Emergency Action Notifications or Terminations (Section 73.922). Those stations which are authorized to participate in the EBS, upon receipt of an EAN (Emergency Action Notification) immediately begin operation in accordance with the terms of their operating instructions as prescribed by the National Defense Emergency Authorization. All other stations must observe radio silence (Section 73.923).

7. **EANS test:** Emergency Action Notification System Tests are made at regular intervals. A test involving the transmission of the Emergency Action Notification Attention Signal and Test Message is made by the radio station once each week (on an unscheduled basis) between 8:30 AM and local sunset. The following steps are taken:

1. Make the following announcement: "This is a test. For the next 60 seconds this station will conduct a test of the Emergency Broadcast System. This is only a test."

2. Cut the transmitter carrier for five seconds.

3. Return the carrier to the air for five seconds.

4. Cut the transmitter carrier for five seconds.

5. Return the carrier to the air.

6. Broadcast the 1000-cycle steady tone for 15 seconds.

7. Make the following announcement: "This has been a test of the Emergency Broadcast System. If this had been an actual emergency, normal broadcasting would have been discontinued and only designated Emergency Broadcast System radio Stations would continue in operation. You would have been instructed to tune to one of your area stations for official information. This concludes this test of the Emergency Broadcast System."

8. **Tower lights:** Tower lights should be checked at least once every 24 hours to insure proper operation. However, a daily check must be made to determine the on and off times of the tower lights. If the tower lights are observed to be malfunctioning, the failure should be reported immediately to the nearest office of the FAA or nearest air communications station.

9. **FCC inspection:** Upon demand, an FCC inspector must be provided (at any reasonable hour) with the program, operating, and maintenance logs, equipment performance measurements, a copy of the most recent antenna measurement, and a copy of the most recent field intensity measurement.

Of course, there are technical obligations which have to be considered by the announcer. For more information on such rules, I suggest you ask the station engineer. Make it a point to become familiar with the technical aspects of your responsibilities.

Most Often Violated FCC Rules

Maintenance log: Violation includes the failure to enter a signed statement of the required daily inspection, record the required quarterly tower light inspections, enter required weekly antenna base current inspections, enter required notation of external frequency checks and monitor correlation.

Operating transmitter log: Violations include the failure to make entries of required meter readings at specified intervals and log required daily tower light observations.

Station identification: Violations include the failure to identify the station by the assigned call letters and location at the specified intervals.

Program log: Most frequent violations include the failure to make or authenticate sponsorship announcements, enter required details of public service announcements, sign the log and initial corrections and show party affiliations of a political candidate.

Operators: Violations include the failure to have a properly licensed operator on duty, at least a verified Radio-Telephone Third Class Operator Permit that is endorsed for broadcast operation and make the required 5-day per week transmitting equipment inspection.

Station and operator licenses: Violations include the failure to post station authorizations and modifications thereunder and operators' licenses at the principal control point of the transmitter.

Operating power: Violations include failing to maintain the power within the limits specified in the rules, maintain the ratio of antenna base currents in a directional antenna system within 5 percent of the specified values.

Modern Radio Terminology

As the radio business becomes more sophisticated and complex, our vocabulary is increasing rapidly, so rapidly in fact that it's not always possible to keep up with the newly introduced terms. I've found that most radio men are rather hesitant to question the meaning of a word. Therefore, I've compiled a list for easy reference. Some of the terms are quite common and others you may never encounter. However, they are all important.

Account executive: Name generally given to all radio advertising salesmen, or an agency man who acts in behalf of his client with a station.

Across the board: A program or announcement which is broadcast every day of the week is said to be running "across the board."

Ad lib: When announcing or speaking without a script.

Adjacencies: Time slots next to, but not during, programs, such as immediately following or preceding a newscast, football game or special broadcast.

Advertising wedges: Within a commercial message, the product superiority or advantages.

Affidavit: A sworn or notarized statement verifying that a client's commercial appeared or was broadcast at a certain time. Affidavits almost always accompany a bill and are generally used in connection with an agency or co-op bill.

Affiliate: A station which is associated with one of the networks. And, in exchange for a fee, it agrees to carry a certain amount of the network's programming.

Agency commission: The fee paid to an advertising agency by the station for various services performed by the agency, primarily the placing of advertising for a client on the station. Fee is generally 15 percent of the amount placed.

Agent: One who represents talent.

Air check: Tape recording of a commercial, DJ, or other program while it is being broadcast.

Area probability sample: A probability sample for which the sampling units of an audience survey are well defined geographic areas. For example, city blocks.

Availabilities: Time which has not been sold and is available for sale to a client.

Background: Sound or music behind a commercial or dialogue.

Balance: (1) Setting the volume of two or more inputs to achieve proper level. (2) Arranging records in a sequence that will provide an up and down rhythm (fast, slow, fast, slow, etc., hard, soft, hard, soft, etc.).

Board fade: Fading a program, music, or commercial down or up by lowering or raising the volume control pot.

Call back: A further attempt by a survey interviewer to obtain information from a respondent who did not, for some reason, provide information at a previously attempted interview.

Campaign: The total advertising program for a client (radio, newspaper, TV, etc.).

Canned music: Recorded music.

Chain break: A station break announcement.

Circulation: The number of households or individuals, regardless of where located, that are estimated to be in the audience of a radio station at least once during the designated period of time.

Cluster: (1) Pertains to music and commercials. When more than one record is played without commercial interruption, it is a music cluster. (2) When more than one commercial is played back to back, it is referred to as a commercial cluster (or sometimes called commercial set or spot set). (3) When more than one comedy bit is used, it is a comedy set or cluster. (4) A sampling unit that represents two or more elementary units in a survey. For example, if the basic unit in a study is a household, and the sampling unit is defined to be a city block, then the sampling unit is a cluster of households.

Commercial protection: Also known as separation. A specified period of time between the commercials of competitive clients.

Continuity (Copy): The script or message for the client. The written commercial.

Co-op: From the term "co-operative advertising." When a distributor or manufacturer reimburses the dealer for a percentage of his advertising budget.

Copy file: Where all commercial scripts are stored.

Copywriter: Person who writes commercials and continuity.

Coverage area: Area reached by a station's signal or the area covered by the station's signal.

Credits: (1) An acknowledgement for the use of material belonging to someone else on a program. (2) Acknowledgement of the people connected with the production or presentation of a program.

Cross fade: The blending of one sound into another by slowly lowering the volume of one while simultaneously raising the volume of the other.

Cue: The "word" or "sound" indicating that a program, commercial, song, etc., is completed and it is time for another element to begin.

Cut: Another word for "edit," deletion from the original context. Also denotes one selection on an album.

Cut in: The insertion of an announcement into a regular program.

DB: Delayed broadcast, which is taped at one time and broadcast at a later time.

Dead air: Silence.

Double spot: Two commercials back to back. Also called a "short set."

Dubbing: To make a second recording from an original recording.

End rate: The absolute rock bottom cost for a commercial.

Feed: To transmit or send a program.

Feedback: The return of sound from the monitor to the mike which originated the sound; it causes a high-pitched squeal.

Fixed position: Sometimes referred to as an anchored spot. Station guarantees a given time for a client's commercial.

Flight: The period of an advertiser's campaign.

Flow concept: A programming term applying to each hour of the day where everything fits together in one continuous flow.

Format: The uniform arrangement of each element of a broadcast hour or program.

Frequency: (1) Dial position. (2) Average number of times that individuals or households listen to a radio station. (3) Number of times a client wants his message broadcast.

Frequency discount: On many rate cards, the more spots you buy, the lower the per spot rate. The frequency or quantity discount given a client.

Gain: Refers to the regulation of the program volume.

Gross impressions: The total number of times a commercial is heard during a specific period of time.

Hiatus: Pronounced "hy-ee-tus." That period when a sponsor temporarily discontinues radio advertising for a short period of time.

ID: Identification.

Image concept: Commercial where the client name or service is sold, rather than specific items or price.

Institutional: A commercial announcement which promotes the prestige of a client, rather than a product.

Live copy: Live script following a recorded message is called a live tag. Live script read directly on the air by the announcer.

Log: The announcer's bible. The station programming guide and permanent record of the time and nature of each program, commercial, etc., broadcast.

Loop: Broadcast line.

Make good: Either a "freebee" or raincheck commercial. If the station failed to run a spot due to error in programming or the spot was in error when it did run, the station will reschedule the announcement.

Mixing panel (mixer): The board where sounds are controlled.

Mobile unit: A traveling radio control room or a news unit equipped with two-way radio.

Monitor: (1) Loudspeaker in a studio. (2) To listen to a program is to monitor that program.

On mike: Speaking directly into a mike.

Off mike: Speaking away from a mike.

Open end: A client's taped commercial with time at the end for a live announcement.

Open mike: A live microphone.

PA: Public Affairs. A percent of a station's total weekly air time devoted to carrying programs in the public interest.

PI: Per Inquiry. An advertising method in which commercials are broadcast and the station gets a percentage of all money received by the advertiser in lieu of regular rates.

Pad: To add to make a program or commercial longer. A DJ will "pad" to the news.

Participating program: A program in which several sponsors participate. A DJ show is generally a participating program.

Pick up: The point from which a broadcast is originated.

Plug: Mention on the air, a free commercial.

Preempt: When regular programming and commercial time is replaced with a special event.

Premium rate: Additional charge for prime time periods.

Primary coverage: An area where the station's signal strength is 0.5 mV.

Radio home: A family home unit or household with at least one radio in working order.

Rate holder: A commercial which is consistently broadcast on a regular basis, from day to day, to preserve and protect the conditions of a contract. (To keep a low rate.)

Rates: Radio station time charges.

Reach: The number of households or individuals that are estimated to be in the audience of a given radio program at least once over some specified period of time.

Remote: A broadcast originating outside and away from the radio station.

Representative: National salesman who works for the station on a commission basis.

ROS: Run of station (or schedule). Spots are spread out over the entire day or week. The opposite of fixed position.

RPM: Revolutions per minute (45, 33 1/3).

Sandwich: Sometimes called the donut. Live or local copy inserted between a recorded open and close jingle or vocal.

Script: Copy.

Segue: Switching from one record to another without any announcement in between.

Sets in use: A rating service term which expresses the percentage of homes in a period using radio.

Setup: The arrangement of microphones and equipment for a program.

Signal: The electrical radiation emitted by a station, which is picked up by receivers.

Simulcast: A program broadcast over two radio facilities (AM and FM, for example) at the same time. Duplicated programming.

Spec tape: Speculative tape. Commercial produced for a client on the basis that if he likes it, he might buy it. A valuable tool for radio salesmen because a spec tape is a tangible.

Sponsor: An advertiser.

Spot announcement: Commercial or public service announcement 60 seconds in length or less.

Spot campaign: A radio advertising campaign using spot announcements.

Stand by: This is an order and signals that a program is about to begin. In effect, it means be quiet and get up or ready.

Station break: Identification.

Sustaining: Non-sponsored.

Sweep: A music cluster. Generally three or more records played one right after another with no commercial interruptions. It is used to create an illusion of more music being played.

Tag: An addition to a program or announcement.

Tight: A program which 'lows with no dead air.

Time: "Space" or the time needed to broadcast an advertiser's announcement or program.

Time buyer: An employee of an advertising agency who buys time or spots on a radio station.

ABBREVIATIONS

AAAA — American Association of Advertising Agencies
ADI — Area of dominant influence
AFTRA — American Federation of TV and Radio Artists
AP — Associated Press
ARB — American Research Bureau
ASCAP — American Society of Composers, Authors, & Publishers
BMI — Broadcast Music, Inc.
BPA — Broadcaster's Promotion Association
CA — Commercial announcement
CAB — Canadian Association of Broadcasters
CB — Chain break
CM — Commercial matter
CPM — Cost per thousand
CSA — Community service announcement
EANS — Emergency Action Notification System
EBS — Emergency Broadcast System
ET — Electrical transcription

FCC — Federal Communications Commission
FM — Frequency modulation
FMA — FM Association
FTC — Federal Trade Commission
IBEW — International Brotherhood of Electrical Workers
ID — Identification
LV — Live
NAB — National Association of Broadcasters
NABET — National Association of Broadcast Engineers &
    Technicians
NET — Network
O — Other
PA — (1) Public affairs; (2) Public address
PI — Per Inquiry
PSA — Public service announcement
RAB — Radio Advertising Bureau
REL — Religion
REM — Remote
RPM — Revolutions per minute
SP — Sports
SRDS — Standard Rate and Data Service
TWX — Teletypewriter's Exchange
UPI — United Press International
WX — Weather
XMTR — Transmitter

Commercial Portfolio  13

The 20 commercial scripts included in this chapter will enable you to begin your commercial copy file as suggested in Chapter 6. And as time goes on, you can add to them to build your file. The more adept you become in producing a good commercial, the more your stock will climb, not only with the sales people but with your boss. Saving commercial scripts can also be a great time saver. A request from the sales department for something for a particular client can be quickly met by just referring to your file.

AUTO BODY SHOP AND REPAIR

SE: MUSIC — "THE STRIPPER" BY DAVID ROSE

GIRL: ALL RIGHT, BIG BOY, IS THIS THE——BODY SHOP?
MAN: YES, MA'AM. WHAT CAN WE DO FOR YOU?
GIRL: WELL, THIS TOWN'S NOT BIG ENOUGH FOR THE BOTH OF US.
MAN: I'M AFRAID I DON'T UNDERSTAND.
GIRL: AREN'T YOU IN THE BUMP AND GRIND BUSINESS?
MAN: WELL, YES, WE ARE IN THE BUMP AND GRIND BUSINESS.
GIRL: AND THAT SIGN OUT THERE SAYS———— BODY SHOP?
MAN: YES MA'AM, BUT YOU SEE.......
GIRL: THEN YOU'RE IN THE BODY BUSINESS, TOO. AND I SUPPOSE YOU PAINT.
MAN: THAT'S RIGHT LADY, BUT.......
GIRL: MY GIRLS HAVE BEEN TELLING ME ABOUT YOU. AND AS I SAID, THIS TOWN'S NOT BIG ENOUGH FOR THE TWO OF US.

MAN: BUT, MA'AM. WE WORK ON CARS...NOT GIRLS. OUR BODY AND FENDER MEN ARE EXPERTS AT MAKING YOUR CAR LOOK LIKE NEW. WE DON'T DO BODY WORK ON GIRLS, BUT WE WILL GIVE YOU A FREE ESTIMATE. HERE AT _____ BODY SHOP, WE THINK BODY WORK IS AN ART.

GIRL: YEAH, WE THINK SO, TOO.

AUTOMOBILE (NEW)

1ST: PSST. WOULD YOU LIKE TO BUY A THREE THOUSAND DOLLAR RADIO?

2ND: YOU'RE OUT OF YOUR MIND.

1ST: I CAN GET YOU A COUPLE OF HUNDRED DOLLARS OFF.

2ND: YOU'RE STILL OUT OF YOUR MIND.

1ST: IT'S WORTH IT. WAIT TILL YOU SEE THE CABINET — A 1973 (MAKE) FROM (CLIENT).

AUTOMOBILE (USED)

ANNCR: THE AUTOMOBILES AT____DO EVERYTHING. THEY EVEN TALK.

1ST: BOY, WILL YOU TAKE A LOOK AT THAT.

2ND: YOU SAID IT. WHAT A SET OF HEADLIGHTS.

1ST: YEAH, TOPLESS TOO. SOMEONE'S GONNA WALK OFF WITH HER IN NO TIME.

ANNCR: AT _____ EVEN SOME OF OUR CARS GET JEALOUS WHEN A SNAPPY CONVERTIBLE SHOWS UP ON THE LOT.

1ST: REAR END'S NOT BAD EITHER.

GIRL: HUMPH—I'LL BET SHE'S GOT A PADDED DASH.

SE: CAT MEOW

AUTOMOTIVE (USED)

GAL: GEORGE, WE MUST HAVE A SECOND FAMILY CAR.

MAN: NO DEAL, GLADYS. I'M NOT GETTING STUCK WITH SOME USED CAR.

GAL: GEORGE, AT ____ YOU DON'T GET STUCK. THEY HAVE AN UNCONDITIONAL GUARANTEE. WHY THEIR ADOPTION BUREAU IS ABSOLUTELY....

MAN: HOLD ON A MINUTE. DID YOU SAY ADOPTION BUREAU?

GAL: WELL...MOST OTHER DEALERS CALL IT THEIR USED CAR DEPARTMENT.

MAN: ADOPTION BUREAU. I STILL DON'T WANT TO INHERIT SOMEBODY ELSE'S PROBLEMS, BUYING A USED CAR.

GAL: WHEN YOU ADOPT A CAR FROM ____, GEORGE, YOU DON'T INHERIT TROUBLE. YOU GET A THIRTY DAY OR ONE THOUSAND MILE UNCONDITIONAL GUARANTEE ON ALL PARTS AND ALL LABOR.

MAN: SURE YOU DO.....

GAL: AND IT COSTS LESS TO ADOPT A CAR. THEIR PRICES ARE THAT LOW.

MAN: OK — OK, GLADYS. YOU WIN. WE'LL GO DOWN TO ____ AND WE'LL LOOK AT SOME USED CARS. BUT WE'RE GOING TO BUY ONE, NOT ADOPT ONE.

GAL: (SOBBING AND CRYING) OH, GEORGE, SOMETIMES YOU'RE SO SOFTHEARTED. JUST THINK. I'LL HAVE A CAR OF MY OWN. GEORGE?

MAN: WHAT GLADYS?

GAL: (STILL CRYING) DO YOU THINK WE SHOULD PAINT THE GARAGE PINK...OR BLUE?

AUTOMOBILE—CAR WASH

SE: SOUND OF CLOCK TICKING

ANNCR: IT HAPPENS 525,600 TIMES A YEAR. ANOTHER MINUTE SLIPS BY. AND YOU'VE MISSED ANOTHER OPPORTUNITY TO GET YOUR CAR A GLEAMING CAR WASH AT ____. TAKE A MINUTE. AND LET'S TICK OFF THE REASONS WHY YOU SHOULD DRIVE YOUR CAR TO ____. THEY USE ONLY SOFT WATER, TREATED WITH A WAX, TO REALLY REMOVE DIRT AND LET YOUR CAR BODY SHINE LIKE THE DAY IT WAS NEW. ____ TAKES THE SAME PRIDE YOU DO IN SHINING

YOUR CAR. THEIR LOCATION IS CONVENIENT, SO STOP BY. THERE'S NO WAITING.

SE: SOUND OF CLOCK TICKING

ANNCR: IF YOU HAD DRIVEN IN TO——, (ADDRESS) WHEN THIS COMMERCIAL BEGAN, YOUR CAR WOULD BE GLEAMING RIGHT NOW. FORTUNATELY, ANOTHER MINUTE IS ON ITS WAY. ARE YOU?

BANK

SE: PHONE RINGS

1ST: _____ NATIONAL BANK

2ND: THIS IS THE POSTMASTER GENERAL CALLING.

1ST: HOW DO YOU DO SIR. DO YOU HAVE AN ACCOUNT WITH US?

2ND: NO, I DON'T HAVE AN ACCOUNT THERE. I WANT TO TALK TO YOU ABOUT YOUR RADIO COMMERCIALS.

1ST: OH?

2ND: YEAH. YOU'VE BEEN TELLING PEOPLE THAT THOSE LITTLE RED, WHITE AND BLUE THINGS SCATTERED ALL OVER TOWN ARE _____ BRANCH BANKS.

1ST: WELL, THAT'S TRUE. SORT OF FUNNY, DON'T YOU THINK?

2ND: WELL, HERE IN THE POST OFFICE WE DON'T THINK IT'S FUNNY. THOSE ARE MAIL BOXES AND THEY BELONG TO UNCLE SAM.

1ST: OH, WE KNOW THAT, MR. POSTMASTER GENERAL. WE JUST WANTED TO IMPRESS PEOPLE WITH HOW EASY IT IS TO BANK BY MAIL.

2ND: WELL, I'M GLAD TO SEE YOU URGING FOLKS TO USE THE MAILS. GOODNESS KNOWS WE NEED TO SELL AS MANY EIGHT CENT STAMPS AS POSSIBLE.

1ST: GLAD TO HELP, SIR. ONE OTHER THING, SIR, BEFORE YOU HANG UP?

2ND: YES?

1ST: WOULD IT BE OKAY TO PAINT OUR BANK RED, WHITE AND BLUE? TO SORT OF MATCH UP THE MAIN

BANK WITH OUR LITTLE BRANCH...UH...I MEAN LITTLE MAIL BOXES SCATTERED ALL OVER TOWN.

BUILDER

1ST: NOW LET'S GET THIS STRAIGHT, MR. TARZAN. THAT IS YOUR NAME ISN'T IT? TARZAN.
2ND: THAT'S RIGHT. T-A-R-Z-A-N. TARZAN.
1ST: WELL, UNLESS I'M MISTAKEN YOU WANT US TO BUILD A SPLIT LEVEL THREE-BEDROOM, TWO-BATH TREE HOUSE. IS THAT RIGHT?
2ND: YEAH...IN THAT TREE OVER THERE.
1ST: GEE, I DON'T KNOW ABOUT THAT TARZAN.
2ND: WELL, HOW ABOUT THIS TREE HERE?
1ST: NO, WHAT I MEAN IS...THE WHOLE IDEA OF BUILDING A THREE-BEDROOM TREE HOUSE.
2ND: WITH A NICE FIREPLACE.
1ST: I JUST DON'T THINK WE CAN BUILD IT.
2ND: GEE, I'M DISAPPOINTED.
1ST: SEE, WE DON'T GET A LOT OF REQUESTS FOR TREE HOUSES.
2ND: YOU KNOW ANYBODY WHO CAN BUILD ME ONE?
1ST: WELL, THERE'S———. THEY BUILD JUST ABOUT ANYTHING.
2ND: ———?
1ST: YEAH, WHY DON'T YOU GIVE THEM A CALL.
2ND: (TARZAN YELL)
1ST: I SUGGEST YOU USE THE PHONE.
2ND: OH, I BEG YOUR PARDON.
ANNCR: ——— CONTRACTORS AND BUILDERS. WE BUILD ANYWHERE IN THIS AREA. AND WE BUILD JUST ABOUT EVERYTHING.

BUILDING SUPPLIES DEALER

ARE YOU THE KIND OF A GUY WHO LIKES TO PUTTER AROUND WITH WOODWORKING, BUT HAS TO SHOP ALL OVER TOWN FOR A LOT OF THE THINGS YOU NEED?

BOY, ARE YOU EVER BARKING UP A WRONG TREE. OUT AT ———LUMBER COMPANY, WE HAVE A FULLY STOCKED LUMBER YARD WITH OVER A MILLION BOARD FEET OF PINE, MAHOGANY, REDWOOD, FRAMING LUMBER, PLYWOOD, YOU NAME IT. WE HAVE IT. NOW YOU MAY ASK WHY OUR ONE MILLION FEET OF LUMBER ARE BOARD. THEY HAVE NOTHING TO DO BUT JUST LIE THERE TILL YOU BUY THEM. AT ——————LUMBER COMPANY YOU'RE WELCOME TO BROWSE ABOUT AND SELECT ANY GRADE OF LUMBER YOU WANT. OR, JUST WINDOW SHOP. AND BY THE WAY, WE SELL WINDOWS, TOO. REMEMBER AT ——— LUMBER COMPANY, LUMBER IS OUR MIDDLE NAME.

CABLEVISION

1ST: HOW ABOUT A LITTLE WORD ASSOCIATION GAME?
2ND: SOUNDS LIKE GREAT FUN.
1ST: ALL RIGHT. CABLE.
2ND: CAR.
1ST: VISION
2ND: CLAIRVOYANT
1ST: CHANNEL
2ND: ENGLISH
1ST: MORE THAN ONE CHANNEL
2ND: ENGLI?
1ST: I GIVE UP
2ND: SURRENDER
1ST: I MEAN I DON'T WANT TO PLAY THE GAME ANYMORE.
2ND: QUITTER
1ST: YOU'RE WAY OFF BASE
2ND: OUTFIELDER
1ST: COOL IT.
2ND: HOW'D I DO?
1ST: TERRIBLE. YOU DIDN'T GET ONE RIGHT.
2ND: I DIDN'T?
1ST: IN THE FIRST PLACE, CABLEVISION IS ONE WORD. AND IT MEANS YOU CAN WATCH MORE THAN ONE

CHANNEL ON YOUR TV. SO IF YOU'RE LOOKING FOR MORE ON YOUR TV...CALL CABLEVISION. REMEMBER THAT NAME.
2ND: WHAT NAME?
1ST: CABLEVISION. FOR PEOPLE WHO WANT MORE.

FLORIST

ANNCR: FOR LONG HOSPITAL RECUPERATION
NO MATTER WHAT THE RAMIFICATION
INFLAMMATION, DISLOCATION...
LACERATION, INOCULATION...
OR JUST INCREASING THE POPULATION...
FLOWERS FROM ————— ARE THE BEST MEDICATION.
BRING INSTANT JOY AND REJUVENATION
BETTER THAN HOURS OF CONVERSATION.
FLOWERS FROM ————— ARE AN INDICATION
OF A THOUGHTFUL PERSON'S CONSIDERATION
2ND: —————, (ADDRESS)

FURNITURE

GOOD GRIEF. YOU CAN'T BUY NEW FURNITURE FOR PEANUTS. BUT AT————— IT COMES MIGHTY CLOSE. COME TO ————— FURNITURE AND TRY. THE SALESMAN WILL GIVE YOU SOME FREE PEANUTS WHILE YOU LOOK OVER THE HUGE SELECTION OF FINE FURNITURE AT —————, AND IF YOU LIKE, BRING YOUR ELEPHANT ALONG FOR FREE PEANUTS AT ————— FURNITURE. YOU'LL LOVE A—————DEAL. IT'S JUST LIKE BUYING FURNITURE FOR PEANUTS.

GLASS REPAIR

SE: PHONE RINGS AND IS ANSWERED

1ST: THIS IS THE GLASS DOCTOR SPEAKING.
2ND: DOCTOR, I HAVE A PROBLEM. YOU SEE, MY CAR NEEDS A WINDSHIELD-DECTOMY, BUT I CAN'T BRING IT IN FOR SURGERY. WHAT SHALL I DO?

1ST: DON'T WORRY ABOUT A THING. WE'LL BE RIGHT OVER TO PICK YOUR CAR UP, AND WHEN SURGERY IS COMPLETED WE'LL RETURN YOUR CAR TO YOU.

2ND: THANKS, DOC. YOU'RE REALLY A GREAT GUY.

1ST: DON'T MENTION IT. JUST REMEMBER OUR SLOGAN HERE AT THE GLASS CLINIC. GIVING YOU A PANE IS OUR PLEASURE.

MARINE DEALER

SE: SINGING—"SAILING, SAILING OVER THE BOUNDING MAIN"

OH, HI THERE, I'M A CHRISTOPHER COLUMBUS AND I JUST WANT TO TELL YOU THAT IF IT WASN'T FOR ME...AND YOUR MOMMA AND YOUR POPPA...YOU WOULDN'T BE HERE NOW. AND THE REASON I MADE IT WAS THAT I STOPPED OFF AT ＿＿＿＿ AND BOUGHT THREE ＿(BRAND)＿ OUTBOARD MOTORS. AND THEN THE NINA, PINTA, AND THE SANTA MARIA...THEY COME IN A WIN, PLACE AND A SHOW. JUS A LIKE THAT. AND I DON'T HAVE TO CHECK THE LONGITUDE AND I DON'T HAVE TO CHECK THE LATITUDE. JUST THE YELLOW PAGES TO GET THE ADDRESS OF＿＿. YOU'LL SEE A BOATS. MOTORS, AND TRAILERS, PILED A UP LIKE A SPAGHETTI. THEY GOT SOME A GUY THERE AND HE'S A TALKING AND I DON'T UNDER-STAND HIM BECAUSE HE NOT TALK A ITALIAN. I DON'T UNDERSTAND FOREIGNERS. SO GO A SEE THE NICE A FOLKS. NOW I GOT TO RAISE THE ANCHOR... ANA POOP A DA DECK. THIS NO JOB FOR A NICE ITALIAN BOY. I DON'T KNOW WHAT THE HECK I'M A DOING HERE.

MOBILE HOME DEALER

ANNCR: A LOT OF PEOPLE SEEM TO HAVE THE IDEA THAT THERE'S NOT MUCH ROOM IN A MOBILE HOME. HOW ABOUT WALKING THROUGH ONE WITH ME.?

SE: PLAY SOUND EFFECT RECORD—20 SECONDS OF FOOTSTEPS)

ANNCR: STILL THINK MOBILE HOMES ARE SMALL? WALK THROUGH ONE TODAY AT _____ , (ADDRESS).

PARTY SUPPLIES

SE: DANCE MUSIC

ANNCR: TAKE AN AMATEUR SINGER

SE: (SING A FEW BARS OF AULD LANG SYNE)

ANNCR: AN AMATEUR PALM READER AND FORTUNE TELLER

GIRL: I SEE BY YOUR PALM YOU WILL HAVE A LONG LIFE AHEAD OF YOU.

ANNCR: AND SOMEBOBY WHO LIKES TO MIMIC CELEBRITIES

SE: (VOICE TRACK FROM A MOVIE COMMERCIAL— FAMOUS MOVIE STAR)

ANNCR: ALONG WITH A HOSTESS WHO WANTS TO PLAY PARLOR GAMES

GIRL: OKAY, GANG. HOW ABOUT CHARADES— PASSWORD. ANYBODY FOR POST OFFICE?

ANNCR: AND YOU'VE GOT YOURSELF A PARTY.

SE: HAPPY PARTY MUSIC UP AND UNDER

ANNCR: AND THE BEST PLACE TO STOCK UP ON ALL PARTY SUPPLIES, TO MAKE SURE THAT THE PARTY IS A BIG SUCCESS IS _____ . COLD DRINKS, MIXERS, PEANUTS YOU NAME IT, THEY'VE GOT IT. _____ REMINDS YOU TO HAVE A PARTY TONIGHT.

PET SHOP

1ST: DUE TO THE CONTENT OF THE FOLLOWING COMMERCIAL ANNOUNCEMENT, IT IS NECESSARY TO UTILIZE FOUR-LETTER WORDS. YOU MAY NOT WANT TO LISTEN.

2ND: —— IS LOCATED AT (ADDRESS). THERE YOU'LL FIND ALL KINDS OF AQUARIUMS, SUPPLIES, AND FISH.

1ST: DID YOU CATCH THAT? FISH? F-I-S-H. A FOUR-LETTER WORD.

2ND: AND YOU CAN SAVE ON ALL AQUARIUMS, FISH, FISH FOOD, AND ALL MARINE RELATED SUPPLIES. IF FISH TURNS YOU ON, VISIT ——.

1ST: THERE WERE FOURTEEN FOUR-LETTER WORDS IN THIS COMMERCIAL. BUT AS YOU WILL HAVE NOTED, THEY WERE ALL CLEAN. WE DIPPED EACH FOUR-LETTER WORD INTO ONE OF OUR SPOTLESSLY CLEAN AQUARIUMS. —— DEDICATED TO BRINGING BACK FOUR-LETTER WORDS INTO OUR CONVERSATION— FOUR-LETTER WORDS LIKE FISH...SAVE...NETS... TANKS....

RESTAURANT

EVERYONE IS SO DIET CONSCIOUS THESE DAYS. THE —— RESTAURANT, IN A SPIRIT OF HELPFULNESS, WANTS TO DO ITS PART. SO, HERE FOR YOU WEIGHT WATCHERS, THE ——RESTAURANT DIET PLAN. STEP ONE, GO TO THE —— FOR DINNER. I SUGGEST YOU TRY A THICK, SUCCULENT FILET MIGNON. OR MAYBE ORDER THE MAINE LOBSTER. BE SURE, OF COURSE, TO SAVOR THE HOT, DELICIOUS ROLLS WITH PURE CREAMY BUTTER AND THE ICY CRISP SALAD WITH PLENTY OF DRESSING. STEP TWO, SWIPE A —— RESTAURANT MENU WHEN YOU LEAVE. STEP THREE...DON'T EAT ANYTHING. NOT ONE SCRAP, NOT ONE CRUMB OF FOOD FOR THE NEXT TWO DAYS. WHEN HUNGER NEARLY OVERCOMES YOU, TAKE OUT THE —— MENU YOU BORROWED AND LOVINGLY RECALL ALL THE MOUTH-

WATERING DELICACIES YOU ENJOYED EARLIER. THE
VERY MEMORY OF THESE TIDBITS WILL SUSTAIN YOU.
AND STEP FOUR...GO TO THE _____ AGAIN. AND DO
BE CALM. THEY HAVE PLENTY OF EVERYTHING,
INCLUDING MENUS FOR YOUR NEXT TWO DAY FAST.

SUPERMARKET

EVER WONDER HOW THE ——SUPERMARKET MAIN-
TAINS ITS HIGH STANDARDS OF QUALITY? WELL, IT'S
ALL DUE TO THEIR DISCARDER. YOU'LL PROBABLY
NEVER SEE HIM. BUT HE'S ALWAYS THERE,
REMOVING ANYTHING THAT'S LESS THAN THE BEST
FROM THE _____ 'S SHELVES. WILTED LETTUCE,
CRUSHED CARTONS, DENTED CANS, SOFT TOMATOES
...THEY NEVER STAND A CHANCE AGAINST THE
DISCARDER. THAT'S WHY THE _____ 'S MEAT AND
PRODUCE IS ALWAYS THE FRESHEST YOU'LL FIND
ANYWHERE. THE DISCARDER IS CONSTANTLY ON
THE WATCH FOR ANYTHING SUB-STANDARD —
INCLUDING THE SERVICE. THAT'S ANOTHER REASON
YOU CAN ALWAYS COUNT ON BEING TREATED
WITH FRIENDLY EFFICIENT SERVICE AT THE
_____ SUPERMARKET. SHOP TODAY. BUT DON'T
WORRY. THE DISCARDER NEVER BOTHERS
CUSTOMERS.

TIRES

SE: START OF AUTOMOBILE, IDLE

OLD MAN: EH, EH...HI THERE, YOUNG FOLKS. WHY, I'M
AN OLD TIRE. WORN OUT. GOT A COUPLE OF BALD
SPOTS, TOO. OH, HERE WE GO. ROUND AND ROUND
...AND ROUND. WHOOPS, DON'T TAKE THESE BUMPS
AS WELL AS I USED TO. ONE OF THESE DAYS I'M JUST
GONNA GO "BAM." HOPE I'M NOT GOING TOO FAST
WHEN IT HAPPENS. I WISH MY PEOPLE WOULD JUST
LET ME RE-TIRE. EH...EH...GET THAT? REEEE-TIRE.
OH, THERE'S YOUTH FOR YOU. REALLY BUILT FOR

THE MODERN PACE. SO GIVE ME A BREAK...BEFORE I
GIVE YOU ONE.

ANNCR: _____ TIRES, (ADDRESS)

WOMEN'S SHOP

MAN'S VOICE—W.C. FIELDS IMITATION

MAN: MISS COLLINS, THE EMPLOYMENT AGENCY
SENT ME. SAID YOU WANTED SOME FIGURES
ANALYZED. NICE PLACE HERE, THIS _____.
GAL: BUT WE CAN'T USE A MAN.
MAN: MADAME, I'M A QUALIFIED CPA.
GAL: CPA? WE WANTED A PFA.
MAN: THE INITIALS ESCAPE ME.
GAL: PFA. A PERSONAL FIGURE ANALIST.   HERE AT
_____ WE FEEL THAT OUR PEOPLE SHOULD
ANALYZE EACH WOMAN'S FIGURE TO HELP HER
CHOOSE THE PROPER CLOTHES AND LINGERIE.
MAN: SPEAK FRANKLY. I'M A MARRIED MAN. TWICE,
AS I RECALL.
GAL: WELL, TAKE OUR HUGE SELECTIONS OF PADDED
AND UNPADDED BRAS. IT TAKES EXPERT HELP AND
ASSISTANCE TO SELECT THE PROPER ONE.
MAN: A USEFUL SERVICE. YOU MUST SOAK 'EM
PLENTY.
GAL: IT'S A _____ COURTESY SERVICE. NO CHARGE.
MAN: IN THAT CASE, MY WIFE WILL BE IN TO
CHALLENGE YOUR INGENUITY.
GAL: YOU KNOW, YOU SOUND A LITTLE LIKE W.C.
FIELDS.
MAN: NEVER HEARD OF HIM. W. C. FIELDS. WHO
COULD THAT POSSIBLY BEEEEE?

186

Index